PACIFIC NORTHWEST
WILDFLOWERS

A FALCON GUIDE ®

PACIFIC NORTHWEST
WILDFLOWERS

A Guide to Common
Wildflowers of Washington, Oregon, Northern California,
Western Idaho, Southeast Alaska, and British Columbia

DAMIAN FAGAN

FALCON GUIDE ®

GUILFORD, CONNECTICUT
HELENA, MONTANA
AN IMPRINT OF THE GLOBE PEQUOT PRESS

Text design: Nancy Freeborn
Map created by Multi-Mapping, Ltd. © Morris Book Publishing, LLC
All photographs © Damian Fagan unless otherwise noted

Library of Congress Cataloging-in-Publication Data is available.
ISBN 0-7627-3572-4

Manufactured in China
First Edition/First Printing

The author and The Globe Pequot Press assume no liability for accidents happening to, or injuries sustained by, readers who engage in the activities described in this book. Neither the author nor the publisher in any way endorses the consumption or other uses of wild plants that are mentioned in this book, and they assume no liability for personal accident, illness, or death related to these activities.

THIS BOOK IS DEDICATED TO MY MOTHER,

Beverly Helen Fagan, for her constant support and enthusiasm,

AND ALSO TO THE MEMORY OF DR. MELINDA DENTON,

for inspiring her students to be outstanding in the field of flowers.

CONTENTS

PREFACE

The morning light worked its way from the snow-capped peak of Mount Hood, down through the mixed coniferous forests, across the placid waters of the Columbia River, to illuminate the brilliant display of Yellow Bells and Grass Widows on a grassland bench where I stood waiting to photograph flowers.

Throughout the morning I looked down towards the river and felt ancient connections of time and people weaving me into this landscape. I heard whispers of native tribes as they dug bulbs, harvested berries, hunted game, and fished the river. Looking upstream, I imagined seeing dugout canoes laden with the Corps of Discovery digging hard against the wind as they plowed their way toward the Pacific and into the pages of history. I heard the complaints of wooden wheels as immigrant wagons bumped over the stony ground, the shouts of drivers mixing with the bellows of livestock and the laughter of children. I sensed the passage of nations, vying for control of the land. I tried to ignore the modern sounds of progress as trains, trucks, and traffic ground along both sides of the Columbia River Gorge.

At this point, 200 years ago, the Corps of Discovery led by Meriwether Lewis and William Clark traveled past on their way to the Pacific Ocean. They were the first white men to cross the western landscape and reach these shores, but they were not the first ones here. Two hundred years before them, this land offered a wealth of plant and animal resources to the various tribes that inhabited this region and had so for hundreds of years before then. Here they dug the bulbs of the same plants that I was photographing, perhaps even digging in this same meadow.

As the day progressed, I observed the antics of bees and beetles, butterflies and flies as they foraged amongst the flowers for nectar and pollen. I did not know many of these insects, but I was just as fascinated by their array of colors and forms as I was with the flowers they were alighting upon. It was then that I thought about a quote from *The Autocrat of the Breakfast Table* by Oliver Wendell Holmes: "The Amen! of Nature is always a flower." If so, this meadow would get a resounding chorus of them.

Catherine Creek
March 9, 2005

ACKNOWLEDGMENTS

As always, a book is never the product of just one person. I appreciate Erin Turner, editor at The Globe Pequot Press, for the opportunity to work on this book. Thanks to Leah Gilman whose copyediting weeded out grammatical errors and unfinished sentences from this text making it a better book.

I would also like to thank the following individuals who have contributed to my collection of information and plant identification: Yvonne Babb, Chip Belden, Nancy Rerucka-Borges, Gayle Parlatto, Gary Paull, Tom Schindler, Fred Sharpe, Raven Tennyson, David B. Williams, and Berta Youtie. I am also indebted to those early plant collectors and botanists who have waded, and will continue to wade, through the taxonomic waters and provide scientific structure to these masses of blooms. And to my wife and daughter, who either joined me on outings or tolerated my "one more stop" progression, I could not have completed this project without your love and support.

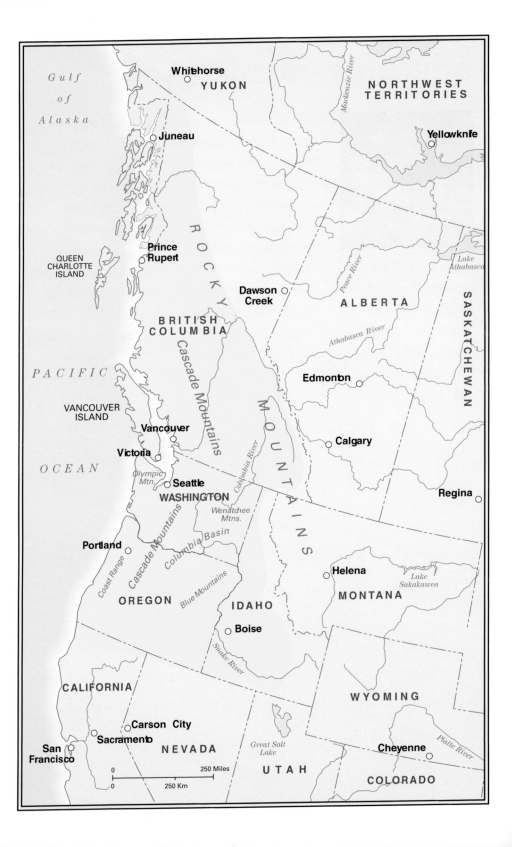

Gulf
of
Alaska

YUKON

Whitehorse

NORTHWEST
TERRITORIES

Mackenzie River

Yellowknife

Juneau

ROCKY

QUEEN
CHARLOTTE
ISLAND

Prince
Rupert

Dawson
Creek

Peace River

ALBERTA

Lake
Athabasca

SASKATCHEWAN

BRITISH
COLUMBIA

Athabasca River

PACIFIC

Cascade Mountains

MOUNTAINS

Edmonton

VANCOUVER
ISLAND

Vancouver

Calgary

Victoria

OCEAN

Olympic
Mtn.

Columbia River

Seattle

WASHINGTON

Regina

Wenatchee
Mtns.

Columbia Basin

Portland

Cascade Mountains

Coast Range

Columbia Basin

Blue Mountains

Helena

Lake
Sakakawea

IDAHO

MONTANA

OREGON

Boise

Snake River

CALIFORNIA

WYOMING

Carson City

Platte River

Sacramento

NEVADA

Great Salt
Lake

Cheyenne

San
Francisco

UTAH

COLORADO

0   250 Miles

0   250 Km

INTRODUCTION

The Pacific Northwest

The Pacific Northwest is a land of contrasts. From dry deserts to moist rainforests and coastal beaches to glaciated peaks, diversity is the rule, not the exception. Influenced by elevation, climate, and soil type, a vast array of plant life forms a mosaic of color and texture blanketing the region.

Boundaries of the region vary by author and, for this field guide, will include lands from southeast Alaska and British Columbia to northern California and east of the Cascade Range through Washington and Oregon into western Idaho. Elevations range from sea level to the snow-capped summit of Mount Rainier at 14,410 feet. These same high peaks influence precipitation as moist air rolls off of the Pacific Ocean and sweeps across the land. Some coastal areas receive over 200 inches of rain a year, while others sit in the rain shadows and receive less than 20 inches annually. At higher elevations this precipitation turns into snow and reaches astounding levels of hundreds of inches per year. Some locations in the region may have scant amounts. Temperatures at noon on a summer day may vary from 50° to over 100° F across the region, and will vary, on average, about 3.5° F for every 1,000 feet of elevation change.

The region's volcanic past (and sometimes present) often dominate the soils of certain regions with volcanic ash and pumice. Both metamorphic and sedimentary rock layers also exist with these igneous types, and their weathering and erosion creates variable soil conditions for plants. Some of these soil types are widespread while others are restricted to particular areas due to the rarity of the parent rock material. On these soil types occur endemics—plant species that have a very narrow distribution but may also occur where different provinces overlap to form unique situations of soils, climate, and topography.

Across the region one can define smaller physiographic provinces, areas united by climatic and soil factors that influence the composition of the plant life that occurs in those provinces. Examples of these are the Pacific Border, the Cascade-Coast Mountains, the Fraser Plateau, the Columbia Basin, and the Basin and Range. One could further divide these provinces into smaller units based upon defined geographical areas like the Olympic Mountains or the High Lava Plains. Familiarity with the plants and animals of a particular province can represent a lifetime's worth of exploration and discovery. But, like seeds carried aloft on a strong wind, we too find ourselves dispersed to other provinces within this region. This curiosity about what is over the next ridge is the basis behind a regional field guide.

How to Use This Guide

There are thousands of vascular plants—trees, shrubs, and flowers—that occur within this region. This book includes descriptions and photographs of 310 of those flowers and shrubs. Representative plants from desert, coastal, and montane areas were selected to provide a general exposure of this vast Northwest flora. There are plants from a diversity of habitats and elevations—sea level to alpine—as well as native and introduced species.

The flowers have been separated first by color, then by scientific family name alphabetically. Where there are multiple species within a particular family, the plants are again arranged alphabetically by genus and species. Some field guides sort the flowers by their taxonomic order, their phylogeny from older to younger. This is the method used in many taxonomic texts, but is exchanged in this guide for this color arrangement.

For each entry there is a common name and scientific name. Carl Linnaeus (1707–1778) was a Swedish naturalist who developed the modern system of binomial nomenclature—this structure of genus and species. Linnaeus created a descriptive system that standardized the terminology and naming of plants and animals, as well as organizing the information systematically. The system provides a common language for all to use. For instance the binomial name *Lilium columbianum* (Tiger Lily) consists of a Latin or Greek generic (referring to genus) name *(Lilium)* followed by a specific epithet *(columbianum)* referring to species. Linnaeus based his work upon that done by various individuals all the way back to Aristotle.

For plants he based his system, known as the sexual system, upon the number, union, or length of stamens and the structure of the ovary. (Because such features do not necessarily show evolutionary relatedness, this has been called an artificial system.) Linnaeus greatly clarified and simplified the identification and description of known and newly discovered taxa.

With Linnaeus's nomenclatural hierarchy, plants with similar sexual features were lumped together into families and then sorted out into finer divisions called genera. The genera were then split into finer divisions of species or subspecies. Today, botanists continue to refine these associations, sometimes moving species around or lumping them together with similar individuals.

This guide includes updated accepted scientific names, although not all botanists agree with those names. Although certain species have valid synonyms, those synonyms have been left out of this guide due to limited space.

The standard field text for the Pacific Northwest is the *Flora of the Pacific Northwest* by Hitchcock and Cronquist. That text is ripe for an updated version, yet my worn and dog-eared copy continues to make trips into the field.

Though there are standards for acceptance of scientific names, such a system does not occur for common names. Thus one person's Tiger Lily may be another's Oregon Lily or someone else's Columbia Lily. Common names are not standardized; thus these can be very regional, best known to the inhabitants of that area.

Under each species is an entry for Description, Bloom Season, Habitat/Range, and Comments. The Description includes information about plant height, leaf shape and size, and flower color and structure. Bloom Season represents the flowering period in the year. The Habitat/Range section is a generalized description of where the plant occurs in the region, in what type of habitat, and at what elevation. These characters may help to distinguish species from others not shown in this guide.

The Comments section contains information about the ethnology or derivation of the scientific names. Oftentimes these names provide information about the plant's physical attributes or about the collector of the new species. Along with the ethnology is random information about ethnobotany, pollination, toxicity, or historical figures in the world of botany and exploration.

A word of caution: The diversity of plants within the region is both exciting and frustrating, especially for the production of a regionwide field guide. It is exciting in that this guide covers a wide area and diversity of plants and frustrating in that there are too many species to include and that sometimes the best level of identification will be a broad one—"that looks like a lupine" or "maybe this plant is in the Lily Family." Nature itself ignores classification; it is we who affix a label on things. That aside, hopefully this guide will be used in association with other books on your shelves that will enable you to better understand these wonderful wildflowers of the Northwest.

A word of encouragement: There is great wisdom in the quote "Stop and smell the roses." Our lives are often defined by time, and there certainly isn't enough to satisfy most of our appetites. At times our preference is to just hear the name of a plant, but not to take a good look at it—let alone to take a sniff of the flower or feel the texture of the leaves. To observe the activities of pollinators, one should take a front-row seat, relax, and enjoy the action. More times than not, taking that extra moment will provide a greater understanding and appreciation of these wildflowers.

Please remember to enjoy the sights and fragrances of these flowers from a distance and to leave them for others, both winged and two-legged, to enjoy. If you are uncertain of the identification create a sketch or take a photograph and write some notes about the plant's features. Resist the temptation to collect specimens, for they may quickly fade and dried specimens are often not helpful for the casual observer to obtain more information. Plus, certain plants are legally protected due to their rarity.

The Functioning Plant

A basic understanding of plant parts and their functions as much to the appreciation of them in their native settings and to identifying them, as well. Roots absorb water and minerals from the soil and transport these to the higher parts of the plant. The stem has conduits for transporting water and minerals to the leaves and for taking products made in the leaves—carbohydrates, proteins, lipids, etc.—to other parts of the plant. Leaves contain chlorophyll and other pigments necessary for photosynthesis. The sugars and other products of photosynthesis and the raw materials taken from the soil are either used immediately or stored by the plant. Beyond these basic structures are the amazing adaptations that plants have made for reproduction.

Pollination is the transfer of male spores, or *pollen,* from the *anther* at the end of the *stamen* to the *stigma,* which is the tip of the female part of the flower, the *pistil.* When pollen grains reach the stigma they germinate, much like a seed, and a *pollen tube(s)* grows downwards into the *style,* the stalk of the pistil. In these tubes the male sex cells or *gametes* form. The pollen tube then grows through the tissues of the pistil. The pistil nourishes the tube as it grows, and when the pollen tube is near the female gamete in the *ovule,* the male gametes release and fertilization takes place. The transfer of pollen to the stigma of a flower is one of the greatest technical achievements of the plant kingdom; the logistics of this have helped create the fascinating variety of flowers we see today.

The fossil record is a stone testament to the innovation of the plant kingdom over millions of years: It reveals spore-producing ferns, primitive fernlike trees that bore seeds; the cone-bearing plants (the conifers); and the more modern orchids with their specialized methods of pollination. Throughout this history there was a noted change from wind pollination to animal pollination, a conclusion based upon the structure of fossilized flowers, which occurred at about the same time pollinating insects became numerous.

Generally there are three main ways ovules become fertilized: by wind, animal, or self-pollination. Wind pollination is considered the more "primitive" form of pollination. Wind pollination is a chancy method and used primarily by plants that grow in close proximity to one another or where there are few insects to do the job. Grasses and many trees are wind pollinated. To increase the odds of pollination, many wind-pollinated plants release tremendous amounts of pollen into the air from their usually smaller and less showy flowers. Some have separate male and female flowers, often arranged in dense clusters, to further this strategy. Some species release their huge amounts of pollen before their leaves develop in order to increase the odds of contact even more.

The evolution of animal pollination, which benefits both pollinator and plant, created a tremendous amount of variation in flower structure, since no single floral type can perfectly suit all types of potential pollinators. About eighty-five percent of all flowering plants are insect pollinated. Differences in flower size, shape, coloration, and arrangement are shown in the simplified chart of Table 2. This does not cover all the groups of insects, and one may observe many different types of insects on one flower.

Most insects move pollen from flower to flower more reliably than the wind. Some insects are generalists and visit different types of plants, not selecting just one type of flower during their foraging. Bees, on the other hand, are more "faithful" as pollinators—they select one or a few species of plants and regularly visit only those flowers, which count on the bees for pollination and reward them with nectar and pollen.

Plants tend to consistently attract certain insect pollinators, and those pollinators evolve to select the flowers that fulfill their needs as well. Nectar, a sugary bribe or reward, attracts the pollinators. Certain plants may time their nectar release to coincide with the times of peak foraging activity of certain insects or birds and thus do not spend precious energy providing nectar to nonpollinating species.

Visual acuity for insects is less than that for humans, and their ability to distinguish shape and form from a distance is relatively poor. Many flowers have developed special patterns of color, called *nectar guides,* which function as landing lights, attracting these pollinators and orienting them to the nectar. Most yellow and white flowers are highly reflective of light and are thus visited by a large variety of insects, but bees frequent blue flowers more than any other insect group.

Table 1. Simplified chart showing some relationships between flowers and pollinator groups (Adapted from Howe and Westley, 1988).

Pollinator	Flower Color	Flower Depth	Odor
Beetles	Usually dull	Flat, bowl-shaped	Strong
Flies	Variable	Moderately deep	Variable
Bees	Blue, white, pink, but not pure red.	Flat or broad tube	Usually sweet
Wasps	Dull or brown	Flat or broad tube	Usually sweet
Hawkmoths	White or pale green	Deep, narrow, tubular	Strong, sweet
Small moths	White or green (nocturnal) Red, purple, pink (diurnal)	Moderately deep	Moderately sweet
Butterflies	Bright red, yellow, blue	Deep, narrow, tubular	Moderately strong, sweet
Hummingbirds	Bright red (usually)	Deep, with wide spur or tubular	None

Plant Characteristics

This section will help to define some of the terms and physical characteristics of the plants in this book. Technical terms are kept to a minimum; for their definitions see the **Glossary.**

Many plants are **perennials,** plants with more or less woody stems and deep or long roots that last at least three years. Two types of perennials exist: **woody** shrubs and trees, or **herbaceous** perennials that die back to underground roots or stems each winter. **Biennials** have a two-year life cycle. The plant becomes established during the first season, often producing a basal rosette of leaves. During the second season, the plant flowers, produces seed, and then dies. **Annuals** complete their life cycle in one growing season, their future housed in dormant seeds. Annuals require specific amounts of winter and spring moisture before the seed germinates; chemical inhibitors within the seed prevent premature germination. In drought conditions the seeds do not germinate and remain dormant, possibly for many years.

Sometimes it is difficult to distinguish perennials from annuals. To identify perennials, look for woody stems; underground structure for food storage such as tubers, bulbs, and corms; or dried flowering stems and leaves from previous years.

Leaf Structure

Important features to note about the leaves and stems are:

- Arrangement of the leaves along the stem: Are they opposite, alternate, or whorled?
- Simple versus compound leaves. If compound, how many leaflets?
- Leaf margin: Entire, toothed, wavy, or lobed?
- Are the leaves only basal or are they also found along the stem?
- Does the leaf have a stalk (petiole)?
- Are there hairs or other projections along the stem or on the leaf surface?

Flower Structure

The diagrams in Figures 4–6 shows a generalized flower in cross section. The variation and number of flower parts are key characters for identification. The **sepals,** or outer series of parts, surround the base of the flower. Sepals are often green and inconspicuous, but they may be colorful and showy as in the paintbrushes *(Castilleja).* Together they are called the **calyx,** which may be composed of separate or fused sepals.

Inside the calyx of most flowers are the **petals,** an inner series of generally colorful parts. Petals also vary in size and shape and may be separated or fused.

The petals are collectively called the **corolla;** some plants, however, may lack a corolla, or the sepals and petals may be identical. Together, the calyx and corolla function to attract pollinators and protect the sex organs at the center of the flower.

Inside the flower are the **stamens,** the pollen-producing structures. Typically long and thin, the stamens have a clublike or elongate appendage at the tip—the **anther**—from which pollen is released. Stamens may number from none to more than 100 per flower.

The **pistil,** or seed-producing structure, has three main parts: stigma, style, and ovary. Pollen reaches the **stigma** or pollen receptor, which sits atop the stalklike **style.** The style connects the **ovary** and the stigma, and is the tubelike structure that the pollen tube grows through to reach the ovary. Within the ovary are the **ovules,** the structures that become the seeds after fertilization.

Here again, variation is the theme song. For example, some flowers lack a style; ovules may vary in arrangement and number, which determines the type of seed or fruit that develops. Many flowers have both male (staminate) and female (pistillate) parts within one flower, but some plants have separate male and female flowers on the same plant or even on separate plants. The term **monoecious** (one home) is used to describe a species where male and female flowers are on one plant; **dioecious** (two homes) refers to unisexual flowers being found on separate individual plants.

Two families with unique flower types are shown in Figures 3 and 4. These flowers are in the Sunflower (Asteraceae) and Pea (Fabaceae) families.

Members of the Sunflower Family (Asteraceae) have an elaborate flower arrangement. A **flower head,** which looks like one flower, is actually a dense cluster of a few to several hundred tiny flowers. The flower head has a series of **bracts,** more or less modified leaves that surround the base of the flower head. The calyx of each of the tiny flowers is absent or reduced to bristles, scales, or hairs—the **pappus**—that form a crown of various characters at the top of the seed; this is often a key in identifying the species. Members of the Asteraceae have either ray or disk flowers, or both, within a flower head. See Figure 3 for generalized flowers of this family. A straplike limb forms the corolla or the ray flower and is usually brightly colored. The disk flower has a small, tubular corolla, usually with five lobes, but with no rays.

Members of the Pea Family (Fabaceae) have a calyx that surrounds five modified petals. The upper petal, or standard, is erect, spreading and usually the longest of the five. The two side petals, or **wings,** closely surround the **keel,** which are the two fused lower petals. See Figure 4 for a typical flower of the Fabaceae.

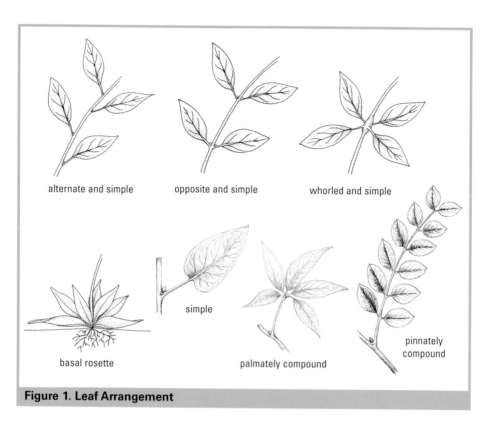

alternate and simple

opposite and simple

whorled and simple

basal rosette

simple

palmately compound

pinnately compound

Figure 1. Leaf Arrangement

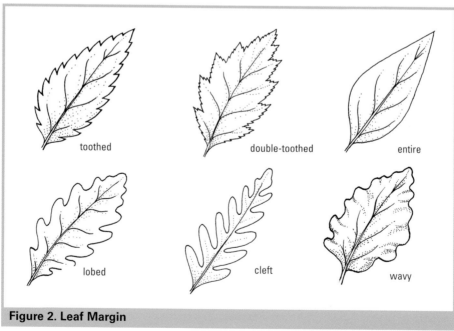

toothed

double-toothed

entire

lobed

cleft

wavy

Figure 2. Leaf Margin

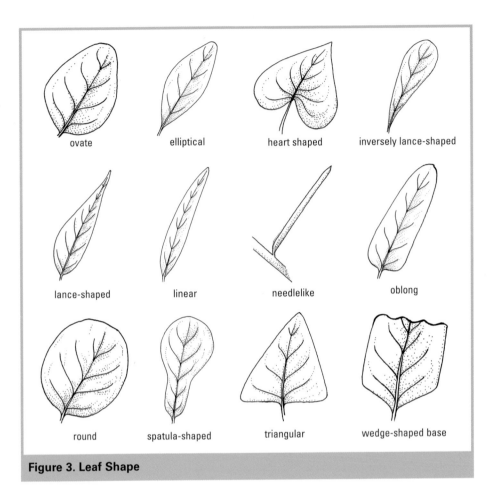

ovate   elliptical   heart shaped   inversely lance-shaped

lance-shaped   linear   needlelike   oblong

round   spatula-shaped   triangular   wedge-shaped base

Figure 3. Leaf Shape

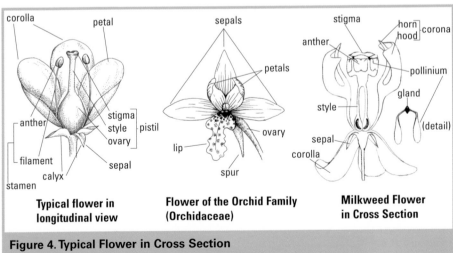

corolla   petal   sepals   stigma   horn   hood   corona

anther   petals   pollinium

stigma   style   pistil   gland

anther   style   ovary   (detail)

filament   lip   sepal   corolla

calyx   sepal   ovary   spur

stamen

Typical flower in longitudinal view

Flower of the Orchid Family (Orchidaceae)

Milkweed Flower in Cross Section

Figure 4. Typical Flower in Cross Section

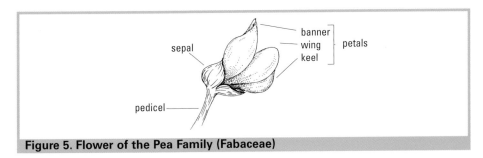

Figure 5. Flower of the Pea Family (Fabaceae)

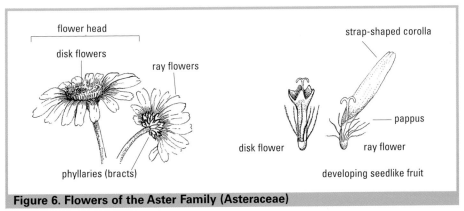

Figure 6. Flowers of the Aster Family (Asteraceae)

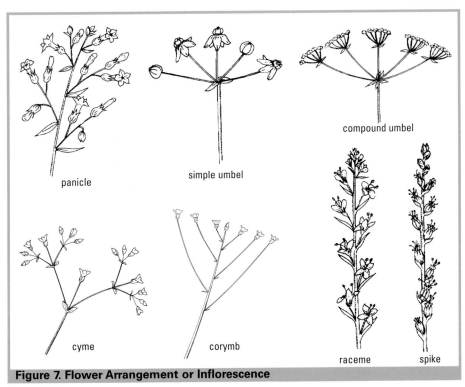

Figure 7. Flower Arrangement or Inflorescence

WHITE FLOWERS

This section includes flowers that
range from creamy to bright white.
Some plants produce flowers that tend
toward pale yellow or pale green. Check
the sections for yellow and green flowers
if you don't find your flower here.

WAPATO
Sagittaria latifolia
Water-Plantain Family (Alismataceae)

Description: Perennial, semiaquatic plant with a leafless flowering stem that is 8–35" tall. Large arrowhead-shaped leaves are up to 10" long, while submerged leaves are either lance shaped or linear. Flowering stalks bear white flowers that are ½–1" wide and have 3 greenish sepals and 3 white petals. These male flowers are arranged in whorls of 3, while the female flowers are ball shaped, smaller, and located below the male ones. Fruit is a sharp-beaked, winged seed borne in a rounded cluster.

Bloom Season: Mid to late summer.

Habitat/Range: Low elevation plant growing in marshes, ponds, streams, and lakes west of the Cascades in Washington and Oregon.

Comments: *Sagittaria* is from the Latin word *sagitta* ("an arrow") and *latifolia* ("broad-leaved") and refers to the large arrowhead-shaped leaves. Native Americans did and still do harvest the thick tubers, which are eaten baked. Native women often collected the potato-like roots by suspending themselves from a canoe and digging the roots out with their toes, then collecting the root when it floated to the surface. Waterfowl and muskrats also eat the roots and tubers of Wapato. The seeds sink in the pond and germinate underwater. *Wapato* is the Chinook word for this plant.

SEACOAST ANGELICA
Angelica lucida
Carrot Family (Apiaceae)

Description: Perennial with stout, hollow stems 4' tall. Compound leaves highly divided. The divisions have broad, toothed margins and sometimes partly cleft segments. Leaves are dark green above and smooth below. Tiny white flowers are arranged in rounded, umbrella-like clusters. Fruit is a seed with side wings.

Bloom Season: Summer

Habitat/Range: Coastal on bluffs, beaches, and wet meadows at low to mid elevations from Alaska to California and along the Atlantic and Siberian coasts, as well.

Comments: *Angelica* ("angel") refers to the medicinal and angelic protection against evil properties as revealed to man by an archangel. *Lucida* ("shining") refers to the glossy leaves. Seeds of a European species were made into gin and absinthe. *Hendersonii* is for Louis Forniquet Henderson (1853–1942), a pioneer botanist in the Northwest and first professor of botany at the University of Idaho in Moscow, Idaho. Seacoast Angelica *(A. hendersonii)* is similar but larger and has woolly undersides on the leaves.

WATER HEMLOCK
Cicuta douglasii
Carrot Family (Apiaceae)

Description: Perennial from a stout, tuberous root. Smooth stems grow upright 20–36". The leaves are highly dissected with egg- to lance-shaped leaflets that are toothed along the margin and have a sharp tip. The umbrella-like flower cluster is borne on a long stalk and lacks bracts beneath the cluster. The tiny white, greenish, or light purplish flowers have 5 petals and stamens. Fruit is a rounded seed with corky ribs.

Bloom Season: Summer

Habitat/Range: Moist areas, ditches, swamps, meadows, and stream edges from low to high elevations across the region.

Comments: *Cicuta* is a Latin name used by Pliny for this or another toxic plant. *Douglasii* is for David Douglas (1798–1834), a Scottish botanist who collected plants in the Northwest for the Horticultural Society of London. The plant contains coniine, an oily alkaloid that is very toxic to people and livestock who consume the roots, young shoots, or leaves.

POISON HEMLOCK
Conium maculatum
Carrot Family (Apiaceae)

Description: Perennial with a purple-spotted stem that is 1–3' tall. The leaves are 2–3 times dissected and fernlike. The large leaves, up to 15" long, are borne on stalks that have enlarged and sheathed bases. Small white flowers are borne in flat-topped clusters. Fruits are egg-shaped seeds with raised, wavy ribs.

Bloom Season: Summer

Habitat/Range: Disturbed sites that are moist from low elevations throughout the region.

Comments: *Conium* ("coniine") refers to the toxic alkaloid that this plant produces. *Maculatum* ("spotted") refers to the splotches on the stem. This plant is extremely poisonous and was administered to Athenians condemned to die for crimes against the state. This European native is now established in the United States.

BEACH SILVERTOP
Glehnia littoralis
Carrot Family (Apiaceae)

Description: Perennial, low-growing with stems sprawling across the sand. The compound leaves are leathery to the touch and have wavy margins. The leaflets may be toothed or lobed, egg shaped and very hairy on the underside. The small, round flower heads bear clusters of tiny white flowers, borne on hairy stalks. Fruit is a cluster of seeds with broad, corky wings (in photo).

Bloom Season: Summer

Habitat/Range: Sand dunes along the coast from Alaska to northern California.

Comments: *Glehnia* honors the Russian botanist and curator of the Botanic Garden at St. Petersburg, Peter von Glehn (1835–1876). *Littoralis* ("beach") refers to the plant's habitat preference. Adaptations to the sandy sites include a stout taproot that stores water, extensive horizontal root systems to combat shifting dunes, leaf stipules that act as sand anchors, and leathery leaves to reduce water loss and protect the leaf from the salty conditions. At first glance the leaves resemble those of the Coastal Strawberry, *Fragaria chiloensis*. Plants bloom in summer, and the wind acts as a dispersal agent blowing the seeds over the dunes.

COW PARSNIP
Heracleum maximum
Carrot Family (Apiaceae)

Description: Large plant, 3–9' tall, with hollow stems. Large compound leaves have 3-lobed segments with toothed margins; each segment is 6–16" long and nearly as wide. New leaves have white-wooly hairs. Numerous small white flowers are borne in terminal umbrella-like clusters. Smaller side clusters contain fewer flowers. Fruits are large, flat seeds.

Bloom Season: Summer

Habitat/Range: Moist sites along streambanks, avalanche slopes, roadsides, or clearings from sea level to subalpine elevations throughout the Pacific Northwest.

Comments: *Heracleum* is in honor of Hercules. *Maximum* ("largest") refers to the size of the leaves. Sometimes called Indian Celery because coastal tribes ate the peeled young stems like celery. Deer, elk, bear, and mountain sheep also forage on the stems and leaves. Hermann Müller, a student of insect pollination, counted more than 118 insect species attracted to the plant's large flowers.

GRAY'S LOVAGE
Ligusticum grayi
Carrot Family (Apiaceae)

Description: Perennial, plants to 30" tall. Stems are smooth and bear leaf sheaths at their base. Leaves are mostly basal, 4–12" long, and highly divided into small leaflets, of which the terminal ones are lance shaped. There are often 1–2 smaller upper stem leaves. Small white flowers, 7–14, are arranged in compound umbrella-like clusters. The fruit is a ½" seed with long, flat projections along the ribs.

Bloom Season: Summer and early autumn

Habitat/Range: Moist or dry open slopes and meadows at mid to subalpine elevations from Washington to California in the Cascades and east to central Idaho.

Comments: *Ligusticum* ("of Liguria") refers to an area in Italy where a relative of Gray's Lovage was first located. *Grayi* honors Asa Gray (1810–1888), an American botanist who wrote *Gray's Manual of Botany* (1848; 8th ed., 1950) and was a Harvard professor. Wild Carrot or Queen Anne's Lace *(Daucus carota)* also has carrotlike leaves and is a very common Eurasian weed that blooms in late summer across the region. Both of these Carrot Family members attract a wide variety of insects to their flowers.

PACIFIC WATER PARSLEY
Oenanthe sarmentosa
Carrot Family (Apiaceae)

Description: Perennial, stems mostly trail along the ground and are 3–4' long. Compound, parsleylike leaves are divided 2–3 times; the leaflets are cleft and toothed, and end in a fine point. The leaflets' lateral veins reach the tip. Tiny white flowers, 5–20, are loosely arranged in flat-topped clusters that are 1–2" wide. A cluster may or may not have several narrow bracts below the flowering head. Fruit is a barrel-shaped seed with ribs.

Bloom Season: Summer

Habitat/Range: Wet sites along streams and rivers, marshes, wetlands, and forest edges at low to mid elevations throughout the region.

Comments: *Oenanthe* is the Greek name for a plant added to wine for its aromatic qualities. *Sarmentosa* ("bearing runners") describes the long runners that arise from nodes where the plant contacts the ground. Although the plant may contain toxins similar to Water Hemlock, some Northwest tribes used the plant as an emetic, for stomach ailments, or to shorten labor during childbirth.

COMMON SWEET CICELY
Osmorhiza chilensis
Carrot Family (Apiaceae)

Description: Perennial, plants 1–3' tall. Basal leaves have long stems while the upper leaves have short ones. Compound leaves have egg-shaped leaflets that are deeply toothed along the margins. The greenish white flowers are borne in flat-topped clusters of only several flowers. Fruit is a club-shaped pod with a pointed base that has bristles.

Bloom Season: Late spring to midsummer.

Habitat/Range: Moist or dry woods, thickets, or rocky banks at sea level to mid elevations from throughout the region and from northeast North America and South America.

Comments: *Osmorhiza* is from *osme* ("odor") and *rhiza* ("root") after the licorice aroma of the crushed roots. *Chilensis* ("of Chile") refers to its cordilleran distribution. Mountain Sweet Cicely *(O. occidentalis)* has yellowish flowers and pods with a blunt base.

SPREADING DOGBANE
Apocynum androsaemifolium
Dogbane Family (Apocynaceae)

Description: Perennial, up to 2' tall or sprawling along the ground. Cut stems exude a white sap. Leaves are opposite and lance to egg shaped and droop from the stem. Small urn-shaped flowers are borne in clusters at the end or along the stem. The white to pinkish corolla is greater than twice the length of the calyx. Fruit is a slender pod up to 3' long that hang downwards.

Bloom Season: Summer

Habitat/Range: Widespread in the United States, mostly on dry soils from low to mid elevations.

Comments: *Apocynum* is from the Greek words *apo* ("away from") and *kyon* ("dog"), although the derivation is confusing. *Androsaemifolium* *("Androsaemum*-leaved") refers to leaf similarity with another plant. Native peoples used the fine fibers of the stem as thread or plaited them into cordage. The plant was also used medicinally to treat venereal disease. Sometimes called Flytrap Dogbane because of the 5 peglike nectaries at the base of the pistil. The V-shaped openings trap smaller flies and moths not strong enough to pull their mouthparts out of the narrow openings. Larger butterflies or bumblebees have no trouble with these openings.

DEVIL'S CLUB
Oplopanax horridum
Ginseng Family (Araliaceae)

Description: Perennial, with thick stems 3–10' tall. The stems have a sweet aroma and numerous ¼–½"-long yellow spines. The large, maple-shaped leaves are up to 18" wide and have 7–9 shallow pointed lobes. The lobes are toothed, and there are numerous spines on the leaf's underside, as well as the petioles. The tiny white flowers are borne along an elongated stalk. The ¼"-wide flowers are arranged in rounded clusters along the stalk. Fruit is a red berry.

Bloom Season: Early summer

Habitat/Range: Moist woods, particularly near streams, at low to mid elevations from Alaska to Oregon and east to Idaho and Montana. May grow at higher elevations farther to the north.

Comments: *Oplopanax* is from the Greek *oplo* ("tool" or "weapon") and *Panax*, which is another genus. *Horridum* ("very prickly") describes the stems and leaf undersides. Native coastal tribes used the roots and inner bark to treat various ailments, the stem wood was carved into fishing lures, and the berries were mashed and used to cleanse the hair of dirt or lice. Charcoal from the wood was added to bear grease for face painting. A tea is made from the leaves to treat diabetes.

YARROW
Achillea millefolium
Sunflower Family (Asteraceae)

Description: Aromatic perennial from 5" to several feet tall. The fernlike leaves are pinnately dissected, meaning the individual divisions on a leaf are again divided into smaller segments. Lower leaves have stalks while the upper leaves are smaller and stalkless. White flowers are borne in large, flat or rounded clusters, and contain mostly disk flowers (10–30) with a few ray flowers (3–5). The tiny flat seeds lack a pappus.

Bloom Season: Spring to fall

Habitat/Range: Widespread from lowlands to high elevations, coastal to drier inland sites throughout the northern hemisphere.

Comments: *Achillea* is after the Greek mythological hero Achilles, who also benefited from the plant's medicinal properties. *Millefolium* ("1,000-leaved") refers to the finely divided leaf segments. Native coastal tribes used Yarrow for poultices, cold and bronchitis treatments, blood purifiers, eyewashes, and other treatments. Yarrow was a parish on the Yarrow River in Scotland's Southern Uplands.

PATHFINDER
Adenocaulon bicolor
Sunflower Family (Asteraceae)

Description: Slender-stemmed annual or perennial that grows 1–3' tall. Stems have dense white hairs below and stalked glands above. Large leaves, 3–6" long, are triangular or heart shaped in outline and may have toothed margins. Undersides of leaves have dense, white hairs. The small, white flower heads bear only disk flowers and the floral bracts curve downwards and drop off when the flowers mature. Fruits are club-shaped seeds with tiny, hooked hairs.

Bloom Season: Midsummer

Habitat/Range: Moist, shady forests from sea level to mid elevations from southern British Columbia to California and east to Montana.

Comments: *Adenocaulon* from the Greek *aden* ("gland") and *kaulos* ("stem") refers to the stalked glands on the upper stem. *Bicolor* ("two colors") refers to the green uppersides and silver undersides of the leaves. Also named Trail-Plant, because the silvery undersides of the overturned leaves create trail blazes. The flowers produce a slightly offensive aroma to attract small flies. When mature, the seeds attach to passing animals and "hitchhike" a ride for dispersal.

PEARLY EVERLASTING
Anaphalis margaritacea
Sunflower Family (Asteraceae)

Description: Underground stems (rhizomes) bear numerous upright, unbranched stems covered with white hairs. These woolly stems may grow 1–4' tall. Numerous lance-shaped or linear leaves bear a prominent midvein and are white-woolly below and green above. Small yellow disk flowers are borne in dense clusters; the white involucre bracts have a dark basal spot. Fruit is a tiny seed that may bear some white pappus hairs.

Bloom Season: Summer through fall.

Habitat/Range: Widespread from lowlands to subalpine regions in open forests, meadows, rocky slopes, and pastures. Sometimes considered a weedy native plant.

Comments: *Anaphalis* is a near anagram of *Gnaphalium*, a similar looking genus. *Margaritacea* ("pearl-like") identifies the shape and color of the flower heads. The dry white involucre bracts retain this pearly coloration when dried, hence the common name.

DWARF PUSSYTOES
Antennaria dimorpha
Sunflower Family (Asteraceae)

Description: Perennial, matlike growth 1–4" high. Leaves are lance- to inversely lance-shaped and covered with dense white hairs. Flowering heads are borne solitary on short stalks; the disk flowers are white to brownish in color. Fruit is a seed.

Bloom Season: Early spring to early summer

Habitat/Range: Dry grasslands, prairies, and open areas in forests from low to mid elevations throughout the West.

Comments: *Antennaria* is from the Latin *antenna* ("antennae") after the resemblance of the flower's pappus (modified calyx) to insect antennae. *Dimorpha* ("2 forms") refers to the plant's different leaf shapes. Attracts flies, beetles, and butterflies as pollinators.

ALPINE PUSSYTOES
Antennaria media
Sunflower Family (Asteraceae)

Description: Perennial, matlike growth. Basal leaves are spoon shaped, woolly on both sides, and ½–1" long. Upper stem leaves are few and linear to lance shaped. Flowering stalks are up to 5" tall and the flower heads have leaflike bracts below them that are dark colored at the tip. Flower heads are a cluster of white disk flowers surrounded by a row of bracts. Fruit is a seed.

Bloom Season: Mid to late summer

Habitat/Range: Open rocky areas or sandy sites at subalpine to alpine elevations throughout the region and circumpolar.

Comments: *Antennaria* is from the Latin *antenna* ("antennae") after the resemblance of the flower's pappus (modified calyx) to insect antennae. *Media* (middle) because the plant is midway between two others with regard to some identifying characteristics. One of several pussytoes to grow in the region.

ENGLISH DAISY
Bellis perennis
Sunflower Family (Asteraceae)

Description: Low-growing, generally 4–10" tall, perennial. Basal egg-shaped to rounded leaves, borne on a short or long stalk, are round at the tip. Solitary heads have white to pink ray flowers and yellow disk flowers. The hairy bracts below the head often have a purple tinge. Fruit is a seed without any bristles or spines.

Bloom Season: Every month of the year

Habitat/Range: Roadsides, lawns, meadows, and pastures from sea level to mid elevations throughout the region.

Comments: *Bellis* ("pretty") refers to the overall nature of the plant. *Perennis* ("perennial") refers to a life span greater than one year. A European species that escaped cultivation, English Daisies are widespread throughout the region.

DUSTY MAIDEN
Chaenactis douglasii
Sunflower Family (Asteraceae)

Description: Biennial, with 1 to several erect stems 4–20" tall. Basal cluster of leaves is highly dissected and may have glandular or dense hairs. The ¾–1" flower heads bear only disk flowers that are white or pinkish. The bracts that subtend the flower head are blunt and have glandular hairs. Seeds are club to cigar shaped, somewhat flattened, and topped with rough scales.

Bloom Season: Late spring to summer

Habitat/Range: Dry sandy or gravelly sites from low to mid elevations from British Columbia to Montana and south to California and Arizona.

Comments: *Chaenactis* is from *chaino* ("gape") and *actis* ("ray"). This name refers to the opening mouth of the tiny, disk flowers. *Douglasii* honors the Scottish plant collector David Douglas (1798–1834), who collected plants throughout the Northwest. Douglas died in Hawaii after he fell into a feral pig trap and was gored to death. Native Americans used crushed leaves as a poultice to reduce swelling. Also called Hoary Chaenactis.

GRAY THISTLE
Cirsium undulatum
Sunflower Family (Asteraceae)

Description: Perennial; plants 2–5' tall. Stems covered with white hairs. The basal leaves are 2–10" long, deeply divided or lobed, and the lobes are toothed or divided with spines along the margins. Stem leaves are smaller. Flower heads are borne at the top of the stems. The round heads are 1–3" wide and have white, pale lavender to pinkish purple disk flowers. The bracts below the heads are brown and lance shaped with spiny tips. Fruit is a seed with fine hairs.

Bloom Season: Summer

Habitat/Range: Dry, open sites at low elevations throughout the dry portions of the region.

Comments: Cirsium is from the Greek *kirsion* ("swollen vein") after one species of thistle was used to treat swollen veins. *Undulatum* ("wavy") refers to the leaf edges. Though many thistles are introduced, Gray Thistle is native. The flowers attract numerous types of insects, especially bees, as pollinators.

TIDYTIPS
Layia glandulosa
Sunflower Family (Asteraceae)

Description: Annual, 4–12" tall. Basal narrow leaves are lobed or toothed, ½–3" long, and covered with stiff, glandular hairs; upper leaves are not lobed. Flowering heads have a center of yellow disk flowers surrounded by several, white, 3-lobed (toothed) ray flowers. Fruit is a seed with about 10 flat, white hairs.

Bloom Season: Spring

Habitat/Range: Open areas and sandy sites at low elevations on the east side of the Cascades.

Comments: *Layia* honors George Tradescant Lay (died 1841), an English naturalist on the Beechey Voyage (1825–1828) who collected plants in Asia, Hawaii, Alaska, California, and South America. *Glandulosa* ("glandular") refers to the sticky hairs that cover the plant. Common name refers to the "tidiness" of ray flowers.

OXEYE DAISY
Leucanthemum vulgare
Sunflower Family (Asteraceae)

Description: Perennial. Stems are 10–40" tall. Basal leaves are spoon shaped and have rounded lobes or teeth along the margins. Upper stem leaves do not have a stalk and are somewhat rectangular. Solitary flower heads are made up of white ray flowers and yellow disk flowers. The fruit is a black seed that lacks hairs.

Bloom Season: Late spring to summer

Habitat/Range: Roadsides, disturbed sites, meadows or clearings at low to high elevations throughout the region.

Comments: *Leucanthemum* ("white-flowered") describes the flower color and *vulgare* ("common") describes its abundance. Oxeye Daises were introduced from Europe and have escaped cultivation and are now widely distributed in the Northwest. The flower attracts numerous butterflies, bees, flies, and beetles as pollinators.

PALMATE COLTSFOOT
Petasites frigidus
Sunflower Family (Asteraceae)

Description: From slender rhizomes arise numerous flowering stems, 5–25" tall before the leaves appear. Stem leaves are small, but the deeply divided basal leaves may be 1' wide. These leaves are heart or kidney shaped, and have 5–7 lobes that are toothed along the margin. The uppersides of leaves are green and hairless; undersides are woolly. Flower heads are arranged in flat-topped clusters. Creamy white ray flowers surround a cluster of whitish or pinkish disk flowers. The lance-shaped bracts that are below the individual flower heads have hairy bases. The ribbed seeds bear a crown of numerous white hairs.

Bloom Season: Spring

Habitat/Range: Low to mid elevations in moist forests, swamps and meadows, and along lakes on the west side of the Cascades throughout the region.

Comments: *Petasites* is from the Greek *petasos* ("a broad-brimmed hat") and refers to the large basal leaves. *Frigidus* ("growing in cold regions") refers to the habitat preference. The common name comes from a European relative with leaves that resembled the shape of a young horse's hoof. The light, winged seeds are easily dispersed by the wind enabling this plant to colonize newly disturbed areas. Blooms in spring before the emergence of the leaves.

WHITE-RAYED WYETHIA
Wyethia helianthoides
Sunflower Family (Asteraceae)

Description: Perennial, 1–2' tall, often covering large areas. Basal leaves are egg shaped and up to 1' long, and have smooth margins; stem leaves are smaller. Solitary, large white flower heads have numerous 1–2" long ray flowers that surround a center of yellow disk flowers. Flowers may turn pale yellow with age. Fruit is a seed.

Bloom Season: Late spring and early summer

Habitat/Range: Often abundant in moist meadows, stream banks, and open areas at mid- to subalpine montane elevations from central Oregon to southern Montana.

Comments: *Wyethia* is for Nathaniel Wyeth (1802–1856), the "Cambridge Iceman" who led 2 expeditions to Oregon in 1832 and 1834. *Helianthoides* ("resembling *Helianthus*") refers to the similarity of this plant to sunflowers in the *Helianthus* genus. The showy flowers attract a myriad of pollinators including butterflies, bumblebees, flies, and Hawk Moths. Also known as Whitehead Mule's Ears after the large mule's ear-like shape of the leaves.

VANILLA-LEAF
Achlys triphylla
Barberry Family (Berberidaceae)

Description: From thin underground rhizomes arise leaf stalks that are 4–16" tall. The broad leaf is divided into 3 fan-shaped leaflets. The asymmetrical segments are coarsely toothed along the margin; the smaller middle segment may be roughly divided into 3 lobes. The tiny white flowers are borne on a leafless stalk and arranged in a tight, 1–3" long spike that rises above the leaves. Flowers lack sepals and petals, but bear 8–20 white stamens. The small crescent-shaped reddish purple fruits are covered with fine hairs.

Bloom Season: Late spring to midsummer

Habitat/Range: From low to mid elevations in shady forests to openings often near streams from southern British Columbia to northwest California, mainly west of the Cascades.

Comments: *Achlys* is from the Greek word *achlus* ("mist") and is perhaps a reference to the misty appearance of the white flowers. *Triphylla* ("3-leaved") refers to the one leaf divided into 3s. To some the lobed middle leaf resembles either a goose's foot or a deer's hoof; hence, another common name for the plant—Deer Foot. The leaves have a vanilla-like aroma when dry or crushed.

INSIDE-OUT FLOWER
Vancouveria hexandra
Barberry Family (Berberidaceae)

Description: Perennial, up to 20" tall. Compound leaves arise on long basal stalks and are divided into 3 divisions that bear 9–15 heart- to egg-shaped leaflets. Flowering stalks bear small, white, starlike, nodding flowers. Flowers have 6 sepals and petals; the petals are shorter than the sepals and have hooded tips. Both the sepals and petals bend backwards and flare open at the base (top of flower). Fruit is a purplish pod with sticky hairs that bears black seeds.

Bloom Season: Late spring to early summer

Habitat/Range: Moist, shady coniferous forests from low to mid elevations west of the Cascade Crest from Washington to northwestern California.

Comments: *Vancouveria* is for Captain George Vancouver (1757–1798), the British explorer who sailed twice with Captain Cook and who explored and mapped the Pacific Northwest coast from 1791–1795. *Hexandra* ("six stamens") refers to the number of stamens. The flowers have 6–9 outer sepals that fall off before the flower opens. The black seeds have a fleshy appendage that almost covers the seed; this coating attracts ants and wasps that help to disperse the seeds. Yellow Vancouveria *(V. chrysantha)* is a yellow-flowered species found in southern Oregon.

SLENDER POPCORN FLOWER
Plagiobothrys tenellus
Borage Family (Boraginaceae)

Description: Annual, with stems up to 8" tall. Basal cluster of leaves have soft hairs and are lance shaped, while stem leaves are fewer and smaller. The flowers are borne in dense clusters; the unopened buds resemble kernels of popcorn. The small white flowers have 5 lobes surrounding a yellow throat. Fruit is a nutlet with a lateral scar.

Bloom Season: Mid spring to early summer

Habitat/Range: Dry, open areas at low elevations on the east side of the Cascades from Washington to Oregon and east to western Idaho.

Comments: *Plagiobothrys* is from the Greek *plagios* ("placed sideways") and *bothros* ("a pit") and refers to the position of the scar on the nutlet. *Tenellus* ("tender") refers to the delicate nature of the plant.

VERNAL WHITLOW-GRASS
Draba verna
Mustard Family (Brassicaceae)

Description: Annual, plants 2–7" tall. The basal leaves are oval to spoon shaped and about 1" long and have small hairs. The ⅛"-wide, white flowers are borne on a short, flowering stalk. The 4 petals are deeply cleft into 2 lobes. Fruit is a flat seedpod.

Bloom Season: Spring

Habitat/Range: Open areas in grasslands, sagebrush flats, or lower elevation woodlands on the east side of the Cascades.

Comments: *Draba* is from the Greek *drabe*, which is the name of a related plant. *Verna* ("springtime") refers to the spring blooming. *Draba* were used to treat infections near the finger or toenails that were called "whitlows" or "felons." Also called Spring Whitlow-Grass or Common Draba.

TWIN FLOWER
Linnaea borealis
Honeysuckle Family (Caprifoliaceae)

Description: Perennial, long slender runners arise leafy stems less than 5" tall. The dark green (above) and broadly elliptical leaves have an opposite arrangement. Upper half of leaf has few shallow teeth along the margin. Pairs of pink ¼" flowers are borne at the end of a Y-shaped stalk. Fruits are small nutlets with sticky hairs.

Bloom Season: Summer

Habitat/Range: Various elevations to subalpine in forests, shrub thickets, or rocky shorelines throughout the region.

Comments: *Linnaea* is after Carl Linnaeus (1707–1778) a Swedish scientist who devised the current taxonomic binomial system of genus and species. In many portraits Linnaeus is often holding a sprig of this plant. *Borealis* ("northern") refers to the plant's distributional range. The common name describes the habit of the fragrant flowers borne in pairs.

MOUNTAIN SANDWORT
Arenaria capillaris
Pink Family (Caryophyllaceae)

Description: Perennial, matted growth. Basal linear leaves often larger than 1" long and end in a soft, pointed tip. Stem leaves in pairs, but shorter than the basal leaves. The flowering stalk rises 4–8" and bears a loose cluster of ½"-wide flowers. White flowers are cup shaped and have 5 petals. Fruits are tiny seeds.

Bloom Season: Summer

Habitat/Range: Sandy or gravelly sites in mid to subalpine elevations from Alaska to central Oregon and east to Montana.

Comments: *Arenaria* is from *arena* ("sand") referring to many species growing in sandy soils. *Capillaris* ("very slender") refers to the leaves; also called Thread-Leaved Starwort.

FIELD CHICKWEED
Cerastium arvense
Pink Family (Caryophyllaceae)

Description: Perennial that grows in tufts or clumps, with stems either upright or trailing along the ground. The upper portion of the stems has sticky hairs, as do the flowers. Leaves are ½–1½" long, mostly linear to narrowly lance-shaped, covered with fine hairs, and pointed at the tip. Whorls of finer, small leaves grow in the axils of most stem leaves. Flat-topped clusters bear 5–9, ½"-wide white flowers with deeply notched petals. The 5 petals are at least 1½ times longer than the sepals. Sepals and floral stalks have sticky hairs. Fruit is a 1-celled capsule that contains numerous tiny black seeds.

Bloom Season: Mid spring to summer

Habitat/Range: Widespread from sea level to alpine elevations on dry meadows and rocky outcrops, but also in moist, open meadows from Alaska to California.

Comments: *Cerastium* is from the Greek word *keras* ("a horn"), which describes the shape of the seed capsule. *Arvense* ("growing in fields") reflects a habitat preference for cultivated or fallow fields and meadows. Field Chickweed is widely distributed across North America.

MENZIES' CAMPION
Silene menziesii
Pink Family (Caryophyllaceae)

Description: Perennial, with sticky stems, 2–15" tall, either upright or trailing. The opposite, lance-shaped leaves are 1–3" long. The white flowers have 5 deeply notched petals and are ¾" long. Fruit is a capsule.

Bloom Season: Summer

Habitat/Range: Meadows, open forests or stream edges from low to mid elevations widespread throughout western North America.

Comments: *Silene* is from either the Greek *sialon* ("saliva"), which refers to the stem's sticky hairs or to *selinos,* Silenus, the intoxicated foster-father of Bacchus (god of wine) who was covered with foam. *Menziesii* is for Archibald Menzies (1754–1842) a Scottish naval physician and naturalist who sailed with Captain George Vancouver on his Pacific exploration from 1791–1795. Carl Linnaeus (1707–1778) concluded that a "flower clock" existed, with various species opening at different hours of the day. The night blooming flowers of *Silene* opened around 11:00 P.M. and attracted Hawk Moths as pollinators.

BUNCHBERRY
Cornus canadensis
Dogwood Family (Cornaceae)

Description: Low-growing perennial. Plants have 4–7 short-stalked oval to elliptically shaped leaves arranged in a whorl or common ring. The 1–4" long leaves are greenish above and white below, with parallel veins. Flower color is variable from greenish white to yellowish to purplish. Fruit resembles a red berry; the red, pulpy flesh surrounds a stony cover that houses the single seed.

Bloom Season: Midspring to midsummer

Habitat/Range: Shady forests at mid to subalpine elevations across the Northwest and south to New Mexico.

Comments: *Cornus* is from the Latin name for the Cornelian Cherry *(C. mas). Canadensis* ("of Canada") is a reference to the plant's distribution, which early botanists used to include the northeast United States. A feature of the *Cornus* genus is the thin leaf veins that will keep connected gently separated leaves. The ripened fruits were eaten either cooked or raw. Pacific Dogwood *(C. nuttallii)* is a tree that has large white flowers arranged like those of Bunchberry.

MANROOT
Marah oreganus
Gourd Family (Cucurbitaceae)

Description: Climbing perennial with branched or coiled tendrils. Irregularly lobed, maplelike leaves are large (up to 10" wide) and have stiff hairs on the upper surface. The male bell-shaped flowers, ½–1" wide and white, are borne in loose clusters. The fused petals (5–8) form a short tube that flares open at the end, often resembling a 5-pointed star. Male and female flowers borne separately but on the same plant; the female flowers are small, green, and inconspicuous. Fruit is a rounded, fleshy melon that may or may not have weak spines.

Bloom Season: Spring to midsummer

Habitat/Range: Open, grassy fields, thickets, bottomlands, and rocky areas at low elevations from British Columbia to California, mostly west of the Cascades.

Comments: *Marah* ("bitter") is from a Hebrew word that describes the flavor of the pounded roots. *Oreganus* ("of Oregon") refers to the type specimen being collected in the Oregon Territory. Native coastal tribes used the plant to treat kidney problems and skin sores. Also known as Wild Cucumber, this plant is related to cultivated plants such as gourds and cucumbers, but the fruit is considered inedible.

GREENLEAF MANZANITA
Arctostaphylos patula
Heath Family (Ericaceae)

Description: Shrub, 3–6' tall. Reddish bark of stems contrasts with the evergreen leaves. Leaves are 1–2" long, rounded or broader at the upper end and often have a pointed tip. Urn-shaped flowers are pink or whitish, ¼" long and borne in clusters. Fruit is a reddish brown berry.

Bloom Season: Spring

Habitat/Range: Open woods, often with Ponderosa Pine, and basalt outcrops on the east side of the Cascades from Washington to California and east to Colorado.

Comments: *Arctostaphylos* is from the Greek *arktos* ("bear") and *staphyle* ("bunch of grapes") referring to the abundant berries. *Patula* ("spreading") refers to the plant's sprawling nature. Manzanita means "little apple" in Spanish and refers to the fruits. Hairy Manzanita *(A. columbiana)* grows on the west side of the Cascades. Northwest tribes consumed the mealy berries. Manzanita often colonizes burned areas, as its seeds require heat to germinate and sprout from the root crown after a fire. Bees, butterflies, and other insects hang on the undersides of the flowers as they probe upward for nectar.

LITTLE PIPSISSEWA
Chimaphila menziesii
Heath Family (Ericaceae)

Description: Perennial, low-growing, 2–6" tall. Evergreen leaves are elliptical and have a white midvein and fine teeth along the margins. One to 3, ½"-wide white to pink flowers have recurved petals and a stout center. Fruit is a capsule.

Bloom Season: Summer

Habitat/Range: Grows in moist coniferous forests from mid to subalpine elevations throughout the region.

Comments: *Chimaphila* is from the Greek *cheima* ("winter weather") and *phileo* ("to love") in reference to the plant's evergreen leaves. *Menziesii* honors Archibald Menzies (1754–1842) a Scottish naval physician and naturalist who sailed with Captain George Vancouver on his Pacific exploration from 1791–1795.

PIPSISSEWA
Chimaphila umbellatum
Heath Family (Ericaceae)

Description: Perennial "semishrub" with woody base and evergreen leaves. Plants are 4–12" tall. Leaves are narrowly rectangular with sharp teeth along the upper margin, arranged in a whorl pattern and 2–4" long. Saucer-shaped flowers (3–15) hang downwards and are a waxy, whitish pink to rose color. The flowers are borne in loose clusters. Fruits are round capsules that contain tiny seeds.

Bloom Season: Summer

Habitat/Range: Grows in moist coniferous forests from mid- to subalpine elevations throughout the region and Asia.

Comments: *Chimaphila* is from the Greek cheima ("winter weather") and *phileo* ("to love") in reference to the plant's evergreen leaves. *Umbellatum* ("with an umbel") refers to the flower stalks arising from one spot. Also called Prince's Pine.

SALAL
Gaultheria shallon
Heath Family (Ericaceae)

Description: A low-growing or tall shrub, up to 15'. Large, evergreen leaves are egg shaped and shiny on the upper surface, and have fine, sharply toothed margins. Urn-shaped flowers are white or pinkish and ¼–½" long. Edible berries are dark purple to reddish blue in color.

Bloom Season: Spring to midsummer

Habitat/Range: Low to mid elevations from coastal to coniferous forests on the west side of the Cascades.

Comments: *Gaultheria* honors Dr. Jean François Gaulthier (1708–1750), a French botanist and physician from Quebec. *Shallon* is from the native name Shallon or Sabal for this plant. Fleshy sepals form the fruits and many Northwest tribes collected the fruits and ate them raw or dried, often mixed with other berries.

INDIAN PIPE
Monotropa uniflora
Heath Family (Ericaceae)

Description: Saprophyte. Stems arise often in clusters, 4–10" tall, and turn black at maturity. The plant lacks green leaves but has whitish, overlapping scalelike leaves that are narrow to oval in shape. The single 1"-long flower is white and bell shaped and either hangs downward or to the side until mature. At that point the flower points upwards. Fruit is a capsule.

Bloom Season: Midsummer

Habitat/Range: Humus-rich sites in dense, moist forests at low to mid elevations from British Columbia to California.

Comments: Both *Monotropa* ("one direction") and *uniflora* ("one flower") refer to the plant's single flower, while the common name indicates the plant's resemblance to a white clay pipe. The plant lacks chlorophyll and derives nutrients from fungi associated with its roots.

WESTERN AZALEA
Rhododendron occidentalis
Heath Family (Ericaceae)

Description: Shrub, up to 15' tall but often smaller. The deciduous leaves are elliptical to inversely lance-shaped and 1–4" long. White to deep pink, irregularly shaped flowers, 1–2" long, have 5 petals—the upper one has a yellow, pink, or orange stripe or large spot at the base. The funnel-shaped flower has a long tube. The 5 stamens protrude from the flower. Fruit is a capsule.

Bloom Season: Mid spring to early summer

Habitat/Range: Moist woods or stream banks at low to mid elevations from southwest Oregon to California along the coast and mountains.

Comments: *Rhododendron* ("rose tree") describes the stature of the plants and the colorful flowers. *Occidentalis* ("western") describes the range of this plant. The crushed leaves have an unpleasant odor. This shrub is often planted as an ornamental. The fragrant flowers attract various flying insects as pollinators.

BASALT MILKVETCH
Astragalus filipes
Pea Family (Fabaceae)

Description: Perennial, with stems 1–3' tall, often in a cluster. Compound leaves generally with 9–19 linear leaflets; leaflets may be larger towards the tip. Elongated flower stalks bear cream to yellow pea-shaped flowers that hang downwards from short stems. The calyx is covered with fine black hairs. Fruit is a long, flat seedpod that hangs downward.

Bloom Season: Spring

Habitat/Range: Dry areas from sagebrush flats to juniper woodlands on east side of Cascades in Washington and Oregon to Idaho and up into south central British Columbia.

Comments: *Astragalus* ("anklebone") is a Greek name that refers to the shape of the pods. *Filipes* ("threadlike stalks") refers to the thin pod stems.

VELVET LUPINE
Lupinus leucophyllus
Pea Family (Fabaceae)

Description: Perennial, stems up to 3' tall. The compound leaves bear 7 leaflets covered with gray or rust-colored hairs. The pea-shaped flowers are borne in a tight, upright cluster and the ¼"-long flowers are white to pale lavender. Fruit is a hairy pod.

Bloom Season: Late spring to early summer

Habitat/Range: Dry grasslands, sagebrush flats, or open woodlands along the east side of the Cascades from central Washington to Montana and south to Nevada.

Comments: *Lupinus* is from *lupus* ("wolf") since the plants were thought to "wolf" nutrients from the soil. *Leucophyllus* ("white-leaved") refers to the coloration of the leaves. Bees and bumblebees are the primary pollinators of plants in the Pea Family. Silky Lupine *(L. sericeus)* is another white-flowered lupine that occurs in the region.

DUTCHMAN'S BREECHES
Dicentra cucullaria
Bleeding Heart Family (Fumariaceae)

Description: Perennial, compound succulent leaves are almost fern-like as the stems branch several times and the numerous leaflets also divide into many segments. Flowers are borne along side of a common stalk; the white or pale pink flowers resemble a pair of baggy pants. The outer 2 petals have ½"-long spurs (the pant legs) and flaring tips surrounded by yellow (the waist). Fruit is a seedpod.

Bloom Season: Spring

Habitat/Range: Moist woods, streambanks, and from low to mid elevations along the Columbia River Gorge and into the Blue Mountains area of eastern Oregon, Washington, and Idaho.

Comments: *Dicentra* ("two spurs") refers to the flower's "baggy pants" and *cucullaria* ("hoodlike") also refers to the petals. The sealed flowers are protected from the elements and small pollinators. Large female bumblebees can reach the nectar with their long tongues. Plants contain a hallucinogenic compound; hence, ranchers call these plants Staggerweed for their effect upon livestock.

STEER'S HEAD
Dicentra uniflora
Bleeding Heart Family (Fumariaceae)

Description: Perennial, very low-growing up to 4" tall. Basal leaves are compound and highly divided. The segments have various lobed tips. The single flower is borne on a short stalk, is white to pinkish, and resembles a steer's head as the 2 sepals curve outwards like horns. Fruit is a seedpod.

Bloom Season: Early summer

Habitat/Range: Open areas, meadows or from mid to subalpine elevations from Washington to California, mostly east of the Cascades.

Comments: *Dicentra* ("two spurs") refers to the flower's 2 spurred petals. *Uniflora* ("one flower") refers to the solitary flower. Easily overlooked due to its small size.

WAX CURRANT
Ribes cereum
Currant Family (Grossulariaceae)

Description: Shrub, 2–4' tall. Branches and flowers have sticky hairs that are foul smelling. The leaves are ½–1" wide, fan shaped, borne on long stems and lobed. White to pinkish tubular flowers are borne in small clusters, where the sepals are fused into a tube with a flaring tip. The petals are tiny. Fruit is an orangish red berry.

Bloom Season: Late spring and early summer

Habitat/Range: Drier locations in sagebrush and pine woodlands from British Columbia to California and east to the Rocky Mountains.

Comments: *Ribes* is from the Arabic or Persian *ribas* ("acid-tasting") in reference to some of the fruits. *Cereum* ("waxy") refers to the leaves or unpalatable fruits. Pollinated by bees, butterflies, flies, and other very small insects.

DWARF HESPEROCHIRON
Hesperochiron pumilus
Waterleaf Family (Hydrophyllaceae)

Description: Low-growing perennial, up to 2" tall. Leaves have narrowly egg-shaped blades and arise from the top of the taproot. Saucer-shaped white flowers have yellow centers and purplish nectar guides on petals. Flowers are ¾–1½" wide; fruit is a 1-celled capsule that contains numerous tiny seeds.

Bloom Season: Mid spring to early summer

Habitat/Range: Moist meadows, sagebrush flats, and dry woodlands from low to mid elevations on the east side of the Cascade mountains.

Comments: *Hesperochiron* is from the Greek *hesperos* ("evening") and *Chiron* ("a centaur, the half-man half-horse of Greek mythology who supposedly was skilled in medicine ") but the meaning is obscure. *Pumilus* ("dwarf") refers to the plant's stature. California Hesperochiron *(H. californicus)* has a bell-shaped flower with purplish flowers. The Dwarf Hesperochiron attracts flies, bees, beetles, and small butterflies to its opened flowers.

BALLHEAD WATERLEAF
Hydrophyllum capitatum
Waterleaf Family (Hydrophyllaceae)

Description: Perennial, plants are 5–20" high. The compound leaves are mostly basal and borne on long stems. The deeply divided 7–11 leaflets are also lobed or divided. The small purplish blue to white flowers are borne in a rounded cluster, 1–2" wide, and have stamens that protrude beyond the flowers. Fruit is a capsule.

Bloom Season: Spring

Habitat/Range: Woodlands, thickets, and meadows at low to mid elevations on the east side of the Cascades from Washington and Oregon to northern Idaho.

Comments: *Hydrophyllum* is from the Latin *hydro* ("water") and *phyllos* ("leaf") and may refer to the habitats this group occurs in, the fleshy nature of the leaves, or the spots on the leaves that resemble water stains. *Capitatum* ("growing in a dense head") describes the flowers.

FENDLER'S WATERLEAF
Hydrophyllum fendleri
Waterleaf Family (Hydrophyllaceae)

Description: Perennial, up to 40" tall. Large compound leaves, up to 12" long, have 7–15 leaflets that are toothed along the margin and may be cleft in the blade; blades are longer than they are wide. The undersides of the leaves have soft, white hairs. Bell-shaped white flowers arise from the leaf axils in dense clusters. The flowers may have a purple tinge, and the 5 stamens protrude beyond the flowers. Fruit is a capsule that contains 1–3 seeds.

Bloom Season: Late spring and early summer

Habitat/Range: Moist thickets, avalanche chutes, and open areas from mid to subalpine elevations from Washington to California and east to Idaho.

Comments: *Hydrophyllum* is from the Latin *hydro* ("water") and *phyllos* ("leaf"), and may refer to the habitats this group occurs in, the fleshy nature of the leaves or the spots on the leaves that resemble water stains. *Fendleri* is after Augustus Fendler (1813–1883), a German emigrant who went to New Mexico for Asa Gray to collect plants.

SILVERLEAF PHACELIA
Phacelia hastata
Waterleaf Family (Hydrophyllaceae)

Description: Perennial that is variable in height but may grow 25" tall or more. Several stems arise from a woody base and may either grow upright or are semierect. Abundant silver hairs cover the broad lance-shaped leaves that show deep veins. The small white to purplish bell-shaped flowers are arranged in a tight-coiled cluster. The stamens stick out above the flowers. The fruit is a capsule.

Bloom Season: Early spring to autumn

Habitat/Range: In abundance in dry, open sites, often in sand, from low to subalpine elevations throughout the region.

Comments: *Phacelia* is from the Greek *phakelos* ("fasicle") and refers to the tight floral clusters. *Hastata* ("arrowhead-shaped") refers to the shape of the leaves that may have basal lobes. Varileaf Phacelia *(P. heterophylla)* is similar with a single erect stem and some leaves with lower lateral lobes.

TRACY'S MISTMAIDEN
Romanzoffia tracyi
Waterleaf Family (Hydrophllyaceae)

Description: Perennial, arises from woolly tubers. Leaves are kidney shaped to round, with broad, scalloped lobes. Basal leaves are 1–1½" wide and have sticky hairs. Flowers are ½" wide and have 5 white petals that are fused into a funnel-shaped flower. Flowers have a yellow center and rise barely above the leaves. Fruit is a many-seeded capsule.

Bloom Season: Summer

Habitat/Range: Grows on coastal cliffs and rocky outcrops, close to sea spray, from Vancouver Island to northern California.

Comments: *Romanzoffia* honors Nikolai Rumiantzev (1754–1826) better known as Count Romanzoff, a Russian sponsor of the Kotezebue's expedition to the Pacific Northwest. *Tracyi* is for Samuel Mills Tracy (1847–1920), a botanist with the U.S. Department of Agriculture. Sitka Mistmaiden *(R. sitchensis)* is a related species that grows on wet cliffs and rocky outcrops in the Cascade Mountains and Columbia River Gorge.

SLENDER-TUBED IRIS
Iris chrysophylla
Iris Family (Iridaceae)

Description: Perennial, spreads by underground roots and often forms small clusters. Basal leaves are narrow, grasslike and up to 16" long. Stem leaves smaller. The flowers are 1½–3" wide, have a long (2–4") floral tube and have white to cream-colored petals that have dark purple veins and yellow centers. Fruit is a capsule.

Bloom Season: Mid spring to early summer

Habitat/Range: Mostly open coniferous woods at mid elevations from western Oregon to northwest California.

Comments: *Iris* is after the Greek goddess of rainbows. *Chrysophylla* ("with golden leaves") refers to the leaves. The Siskiyou Iris *(I. bracteata)* has white to pale yellow petals that have dark veins and yellow centers and very short floral tubes. This is 1 of 4 white (to yellowish) irises that occur in southwest Oregon.

DWARF ONION
Allium parvum
Lily Family (Liliaceae)

Description: Perennial from a bulb. Flattened leaves are sickle shaped and extend beyond the short-stemmed flowering cluster. Bracts below the flowering cluster are egg- to lance-shaped and pointed at the tip. Individual flowers are ⅛–¼" wide and made up of 6 pinkish tepals that are narrow at the tip. The stamens do not protrude above the tepals. Fruit is a capsule.

Bloom Season: Spring

Habitat/Range: Dry, rocky soil in sagebrush and juniper woodlands from eastern Oregon to California and east to western Idaho.

Comments: *Allium* is from the Greek name for garlic, and *parvum* ("small") refers to the plant's stature. Robinson's Onion, *(A. robinsonii),* is similar and occurs in central Washington to the east end of the Columbia River Gorge.

CASCADE MARIPOSA LILY
Calochortus subalpinus
Lily Family (Liliaceae)

Description: Perennial to 15" tall. The grasslike leaves arise basely from the stem, are flattened and about as long as the flowering stalk. Stems bear 1–5 flowers that arise from the same point. Flowers are 1½–2" wide, yellowish white (centers are yellow), and fringed with fine hairs. Petals often have a narrow purple crescent gland low on the petal and the sepals have a purple dot at their base. Fruit is a 3-winged capsule that hangs downwards.

Bloom Season: Summer

Habitat/Range: Dry meadows, volcanic soils, and open forests from mid to subalpine elevations in the Cascade Mountains from southern Washington to central Oregon.

Comments: *Calochortus* ("beautiful grass") describes the leaves of this genus and *subalpinus* ("subalpine") defines the elevational distribution of this species. Also called Cat's Ear Lily after the resemblance of the hairy fringe on the petals to that of a feline's ear.

QUEEN'S CUP
Clintonia uniflora
Lily Family (Liliaceae)

Description: Perennial. several broad elliptical to oblong leaves, generally 3–7" long, arise from an underground stem (rhizome). The leaves have hairy margins and end in a pointed or rounded tip. A single (rarely 2) white, cup-shaped flower arises on a long stalk. The 1"-wide flower has 6 petal-like tepals. Fruit is a blue, beadlike berry.

Bloom Season: Early to midsummer

Habitat/Range: Mostly in moist coniferous forests from low to subalpine elevation from Alaska to California and east to Montana.

Comments: *Clintonia* honors De Witt Clinton (1769–1828) a former New York state senator, mayor of New York City, presidential candidate (Peace Party in 1812), and governor of New York, who also wrote natural history books. His political support of the Erie Canal led doubters to label it "Clinton's Ditch." *Uniflora* ("one flower") refers to the single flower. Also known as Blue-Bead Lily after the fruit, which grouse consume.

OREGON TROUT LILY

Erythronium oregonum
Lily Family (Liliaceae)

Description: Perennial, plants are 6–12" tall. The pair of basal leaves are broadly elliptical to lance shaped and 5–8" long, and often have pale green, purple, or brown mottling. A single (sometimes 2 or more) nodding flower is borne on a long, 7–13" flowering stalk. The similar white to cream-colored petals and sepals curve backwards with age and have an orange-yellow blotch at their base. The flowers are 1–6" wide. Fruit is a capsule.

Bloom Season: Early to mid spring

Habitat/Range: Well-drained moist sites in open or dense forests, fields, rocky slopes, and meadows at low (mostly) to mid elevations from British Columbia to southwest Oregon on the west side of the Cascades.

Comments: *Erythronium* is from the Greek *erythros* ("red") and refers to a red dye made from a pinkish-flowered relative. *Oregonum* ("of Oregon") refers to the type locality. The roots were eaten either raw or cooked by native tribes, as well as bears that may consume the whole plant. Though the flowers are very showy, there may be small pollinators such as beetles or flies crawling around inside the flowers. Pink Fawn Lily, *(E. revolutum),* is similar but has pink flowers and a more coastal distribution. Also Called Giant Dog-Tooth Lily; Lamb's-, Deer's-, or Adder's-Tongue; or White Fawn Lily.

47

SAND LILY
Leucocrinum montanum
Lily Family (Liliaceae)

Description: Perennial, from deeply buried roots. The numerous straplike leaves arise from the top of the root as these plants lack stems. The tufted leaves are up to 10" long and have a whitish margin. The fragrant flowers are borne on stalks, 2–5" long, that may barely rise above the ground. The showy white flowers are often borne in clusters; individual flowers are 1–2" across. Fruit is an egg-shaped capsule.

Bloom Season: Spring

Habitat/Range: Sandy or rocky soils in sagebrush flats and open woodlands from low to mid elevations from Oregon to California and east to South Dakota.

Comments: *Leucocrinum* is from the Greek *leukos* ("white") and *crinon* ("lily"), while *montanum* ("of the mountains") refers to the plant's distribution. Plants may lie dormant during dry years.

CASCADES LILY
Lilium washingtonianum
Lily Family (Liliaceae)

Description: Perennial, from 2–6' tall. The 2–4" long, lance-shaped leaves are arranged alternately on the lower stem and have wavy margins. Upper stem leaves arise in a whorled pattern and are smaller. The fragrant, 2–4" long flowers are bell shaped and have white to pale pink tepals with purplish spots that fade to pink or purple when mature. Fruit is a capsule.

Bloom Season: Early summer

Habitat/Range: Open forests or clearings at mid elevations in the Oregon and California Cascades.

Comments: *Lilium* is the Latin name for this genus, and *washingtonianum* is for Martha Washington. These plants resemble the cultivated Easter Lily; indiscriminate collecting has made this species difficult to locate.

FALSE LILY-OF-THE-VALLEY
Maianthemum dilatatum
Lily Family (Liliaceae)

Description: Perennial, often found in dense clusters as the plants sprout from underground lateral roots. Each plant bears 1–3, heart-shaped, glossy leaves that may be 5" long. Floral stalks arise above the leaves and bear a cluster of small white flowers; floral parts are in 4s (instead of the usual 3 for Liliaceae members). Fruit is a light green to mottled brown berry that turns red with age.

Bloom Season: Spring

Habitat/Range: From low to mid elevations in moist, shady forests, along streambanks, and under Sitka spruce forests near the coast.

Comments: *Maianthemum* is from the Greek *maios* ("May") and *anthemon* ("flower"), which reflects the plant's springtime blooming. *Dilatatum* ("expanding") refers to the sprouting from the roots. Native coastal tribes used the plant medicinally to treat wounds, eyestrain, and internal injuries.

FALSE SOLOMON'S-SEAL
Maianthemum racemosa
Lily Family (Liliaceae)

Description: Perennial, often in clumps, with upright or arched stems, 1–3' long. Broad, egg-shaped leaves are 3–10" long. Numerous, tiny white flowers borne in a terminal cluster. Individual flowers of 6 distinct tepals. Fruits are fleshy red berries that may have purple spots.

Bloom Season: Spring to early summer

Habitat/Range: Grows in moist woods, meadows, and along streambanks from low to mid elevations throughout the region.

Comments: *Maianthemum* is from the Greek *maios* ("May") and *anthemon* ("flower"), which reflects the plant's springtime blooming. *Racemosa* ("flowers in a raceme") describes the floral arrangement. Native Northwest tribes used the boiled roots as either a tea for rheumatism, back injuries, or kidney problems or as a poultice for wounds. Although the berries are nontoxic and eaten by wildlife, they are poor tasting.

STAR-FLOWERED FALSE SOLOMON'S-SEAL
Maianthemum stellata
Lily Family (Liliaceae)

Description: Perennial with upright or arched stems 10–30" tall. Broad lance-shaped leaves are 2½–8" long. Five to 10, white, starlike flowers are borne in an unbranched terminal cluster. The fruit is a greenish yellow berry with 3 or 6 bluish purple stripes that darken with age.

Bloom Season: Spring to midsummer

Habitat/Range: Moist woodlands and streambanks or drier meadows and clearings from low to high elevations throughout the region.

Comments: *Maianthemum* is from the Greek *maios* ("May") and *anthemon* ("flower"), which reflects the plant's springtime blooming. *Stellata* ("starlike") refers to the flowers. The berries are edible, but of poor quality. This species and *M. racemosa* resemble *Polygonatum multiflorum* (Solomon's-Seal) hence the "false" title.

HOOKER'S FAIRY BELL
Prosartes hookeri
Lily Family (Liliaceae)

Description: Plants 1–3' tall with few branches. Stalkless leaves are broadly lance-shaped to oval, slightly hairy, with pointed tips and wavy margins. The ¾"-long, greenish white bell-shaped flowers are borne mostly in pairs and hang downwards. Flowers flare open at the end. Fruit is a yellowish to red, oval berry.

Bloom Season: Late spring to midsummer

Habitat/Range: Dense, moist woods or mixed forests at low elevations from British Columbia to western Montana and to the Cascades in northern Oregon.

Comments: *Prosartes* ("attached") refers to the flowers. *Hookeri* honors Joseph Hooker (1817–1911), a widely traveled British plant hunter and explorer. The common name describes the fairylike quality of the flowers.

SMITH'S FAIRYBELL
Prosartes smithii
Lily Family (Liliaceae)

Description: Perennial, 1–3' tall, with numerous branches and smooth stems and leaves. Leaf bases clasp the stem. The 2–5" long leaves are broadly lance-shaped and pointed at the tip. Bell-shaped, 1"-long flowers hang downwards and are arranged in groups. The cream-colored tepals do not flare open to expose the stamens. Fruit is a yellowish to orange-red berry.

Bloom Season: Late spring to midsummer

Habitat/Range: Moist sites in woods and along streambanks from British Columbia to California in the Coast Range and west slope of the Cascades.

Comments: *Prosartes* ("attached") refers to the flowers. Common and specific name honors Sir James E. Smith (1759–1828), an English botanist who purchased the Linnaeus collection and later formed the prestigious Linnean Society of London.

TWISTED FLOWER
Streptopus amplexifolius
Lily Family (Liliaceae)

Description: Perennial, 1–3' tall. Branched stems are bent in zigzag patterns. Egg- to lance-shaped leaves are 2–6" long and clasp the stem. Whitish bell-shaped flowers are green-tinged with flaring tips and are borne on twisted stalks below a leaf. Fruit is a translucent yellow to red berry that may darken at maturity.

Bloom Season: Summer

Habitat/Range: Moist sites along streambanks, clearings, and thickets in forests in subalpine elevations from Alaska to California and east through much of Canada and the northern United States.

Comments: *Streptopus* ("twisted foot") refers to the flower stalks twisting beneath the leaf. *Amplexifolius* ("stem-clasping leaf") refers to the way the leaf attaches to the stem. Rosy Twisted-Stalk *(S. roseus)* is similar in appearance but with rosy flowers with magenta spots. The edible fruits reportedly taste like cucumbers.

STICKY TOFIELDIA
Tofieldia glutinosa
Lily Family (Liliaceae)

Description: Perennial, with stems 4–20" tall. One to 3 grasslike leaves, 3–7" long, form a basal clump. The floral stem is hairy and very sticky on the upper portion and may bear 1–2 smaller leaves. The small, ¼"-wide, white to greenish white flowers are arranged in dense clusters at the tip of the leafless floral stalk. The dark "spots" on the tepals are the stamens. The fruit is a membranous reddish purple capsule with spongy seeds.

Bloom Season: Early to midsummer

Habitat/Range: Wet meadows, bogs, marshes, and streambanks at low to alpine elevations from Alaska to California and east to the Rocky Mountains.

Comments: Named for Thomas Tofield (1730–1799), a British botanist. *Glutinosa* ("glutinous") refers to the sticky hairs on the stems. Also called False Asphodel (after another genus in the lily family *Asphodeline*), and identified as the flower of the dead in Homer's Elysian Fields. Attracts small flies as pollinators.

WESTERN TRILLIUM
Trillium ovatum
Lily Family (Liliaceae)

Description: From a fleshy rhizome arises a single hairless stem that bears large leaves shaped like rounded-edge triangles in whorls of 3 (may be up to 5). Stalkless leaves (sessile) are dark green and not mottled. Normally a single white, turning pink to purplish with age, flower is borne at the end of a short stalk. The 3 flower petals may be up to 5 cm long. Fruits are a many-seeded, berrylike capsule.

Bloom Season: Springtime

Habitat/Range: Prefers moist open forests and boggy areas from lowland to high elevations from British Columbia to central California and east to the Rocky Mountains.

Comments: *Trillium* ("in 3s"), refers to the number of leaves and floral parts. *Ovatum* ("oval-like") refers to the leaf shape. Ants collect the seeds and eat the oil-rich appendage on the tip. Discarded seeds may sprout to form future plants, although it takes 6–8 years from germination to flowering. Sessile or Giant Trillium *(T. chloropetalum)* has stalkless, mottled leaves and greenish white to pink or deep purple flowers. Trilliums are also called Wake-Robin for their springtime appearance, which coincides with the territorial singing of robins.

HYACINTH BRODIAEA
Triteleia hyacinthium
Lily Family (Liliaceae)

Description: Perennial, plants 1–2' tall. The grasslike leaves are longer than the flowering stem but wither at flowering. Dense clusters of white flowers are borne in an umbrella-like pattern. The tepals form a short tube with flaring lobes; the lobes have a green midline. Flowers are ½–¾" long. Fruit is a capsule.

Bloom Season: Mid spring to early summer

Habitat/Range: Meadows, grasslands, and sagebrush flats at low elevations.

Comments: *Triteleia* is from the Greek *tri* ("three") and *teleios* ("perfect") in reference to the floral parts in 3s. *Hyacinthium* ("resembling a hyacinth") refers to the resemblance of the flowers to those of hyacinths. Also called Fool's Onion because the edible bulbs lack an onion odor.

GREEN FALSE HELLEBORE
Veratrum viride
Lily Family (Liliaceae)

Description: Perennial, grows 3–6' from thick rhizomes. Large oval to inversely lance-shaped leaves are 10–14" long at the base of the flowering stem, and smaller up towards the top. Small flowers arranged in an elongated cluster, the flower branches droop. Individual flowers are ¼–½" wide and have 6 tepals. The mature capsule contains numerous winged, papery seeds.

Bloom Season: Summer to fall

Habitat/Range: Moist and wet areas from lowlands to subalpine forests from Alaska to eastern Canada and south to Oregon and Idaho. Also occurs in North Carolina.

Comments: *Veratrum* is from the Latin words *vere* ("true") and *ater* ("black") after the black roots of another species. False Hellebore *(V. californica)* is somewhat similar but with nondropping flowering branches. Toxic to livestock, at one time an insecticide was made from the powdered roots.

BEARGRASS
Xerophyllum tenax
Lily Family (Liliaceae)

Description: Perennial, growing 2–5' tall. Evergreen basal leaves, up to 3' long, grow in clumps and are grasslike with fine-toothed edges. The stem leaves are similar but smaller progressively up the stem. Cream-colored flowers borne in dense clusters called racemes at the end of the flowering stalk. The individual flowers are borne on long stems, have 6 tepals and are fragrant. The fruit is a capsule.

Bloom Season: Summer

Habitat/Range: From sea level to subalpine elevations and found in meadows, clearings, or the undergrowth of open to dense forests from British Columbia to California and east to Wyoming.

Comments: *Xerophyllum* is from the Greek *xeros* ("dry") and *phylum* ("leaf"), and *tenax* ("tough"). Native peoples wove the tough leaves into durable capes, baskets, or hats; even Lewis and Clark had Beargrass rain hats made for their crew. In spring bears consume the softer, fleshy leaf bases; hence the common name reference.

PANICLED DEATH CAMAS

Zygadenus paniculatus
Lily Family (Liliaceae)

Description: Perennial, from a bulb with slender stems 20" high. Basal leaves are straplike and up to ½" wide. The flower heads are arranged in a loose cluster with the younger flowers at the top or middle. The whitish ¼"-wide flowers are borne on small stalks along side branches of the main flowering stalk. Flowers made up of 6 tepals each bearing a yellowish green egg-shaped gland. Fruit is a capsule.

Bloom Season: Spring

Habitat/Range: Open meadows, sagebrush flats, open ponderosa, or lodgepole woodlands from eastern Washington to southern Idaho and south to California.

Comments: *Zygadenus* is from the Greek *zugon* ("yoke") and *aden* ("gland") referring to the yoked or joined nectar glands found on the tepals. *Paniculatus* ("flowers in a panicle") describes the arrangement of the flowers. Death Camas contains toxic alkaloids; hence, the native tribes had to be careful when digging the edible Camas bulbs *(Camassia quamash)*, which may grow intermixed with Death Camas.

POISON DEATH CAMAS
Zygadenus venenosus
Lily Family (Liliaceae)

Description: Perennial, from an onionlike bulb arise grasslike, linear leaves up to 15" long. Tiny creamy white flowers are borne on short stalks in a pyramid-shaped cluster. Tepals are shorter than the stamens and have a greenish, oval dot at the base. Flowers have a strong aroma. Fruit is a narrow capsule.

Bloom Season: Mid spring to midsummer

Habitat/Range: Rocky or grassy slopes, open forests, meadows (dry in summer), and forest edges from low to mid elevations from British Columbia to California.

Comments: *Zygadenus* is from the Greek *zugon* ("yoke") and *aden* ("gland") referring to the yoked or joined nectar glands found on the tepals. *Venenosus* ("poisonous") refers to the bulbs, which contain toxic alkaloids. Mountain Death Camas *(Z. elegans)* has larger flowers also arranged in a raceme and each tepal bears a green heart-shaped gland. Meriwether Lewis collected this Death Camas on July 7, 1806, near the present-day Lewis and Clark Pass in Montana.

SAND VERBENA
Abronia fragrans
Four O'Clock Family (Nyctaginaceae)

Description: Perennial, with stems 7–32" long. The stems are smooth or covered with sticky hairs that may have attached sand grains. The lance- to egg-shaped leaves are ⅜–3½" long and also covered with fine sticky hairs. The tubular white flowers are borne in dense, rounded clusters of 25–80 flowers. Individual flowers are ⅜–1" long and the lobed ends are wavy along the edge. Fruit is a winged seed.

Bloom Season: Late spring

Habitat/Range: Sandy sites at low elevation from Idaho's Snake River Plains to the Rocky Mountains.

Comments: *Abronia* is from the Greek *abros* ("graceful") and refers to the flowers, while *fragrans* ("fragrant") reveals their aroma. These flowers open in the evening and attract Hawk Moths as pollinators, and butterflies are attracted to the flowers before they close in the morning. White Sand Verbena *(A. mellifera)* is similar but with thin wings on the seeds, smaller flowering head bracts and scarcely fragrant flowers. This species occurs in eastern Washington and Oregon into the Snake River Plain.

AMERICAN WATER-LILY
Nymphaea odorata
Water-Lily Family (Nymphaeaceae)

Description: Aquatic perennial. Large padlike leaves are up to 13" wide and have a cleft near their stem that keeps them from being round. The showy flowers are 1½–4" wide and have many white (sometimes pinkish) petals and numerous stamens and pistils. Fruit is a leathery capsule.

Bloom Season: Midsummer to fall

Habitat/Range: Lowland lakes on both sides of the Cascades; introduced from eastern North America.

Comments: *Nymphaea* ("water nymph") refers to the plant's aquatic habitat and nymphlike pure white petals. *Odorata* ("scented") refers to the sweet smell of the flowers. Eastern tribes ate the leaves, flower buds, roots, and capsules, and used the plant for its medicinal qualities of treating internal disorders. The flowers, which open in the morning and close in the afternoon, contain no nectar; however, beetles are attracted to the flowers for the abundant pollen.

SPREADING GAYOPHYTUM
Gayophytum diffusum
Evening Primrose Family (Onagraceae)

Description: Annual, with branched slender stems up to 3' tall. Narrow linear leaves, ½–1" long are shorter than the distance between 2 nodes along the stem. Flowers are ⅛–¼" wide, with 4 white petals and 8 stamens. Fruit is a slender, upright or spreading capsule.

Bloom Season: Summer

Habitat/Range: Dry soils in open valleys and woodlands from low to subalpine elevations across much of western United States.

Comments: *Gayophytum* is for Claude Gay (1800–1873), a French botanist who wrote the *Flora of Chile*. *Diffusum* ("spreading") indicates the growth habit of this almost weedy species. Hairstem Gayophytum *(G. ramosissima)* has smaller flowers and capsules that also angle downwards.

DWARF EVENING PRIMROSE
Oenothera caespitosa
Evening Primrose Family (Onagraceae)

Description: Low-growing perennial with long-stalked lance- to inversely lance-shaped leaves that are up to 8" long. Leaf margins variable from entire to deeply lobed. White flowers are 2–4" wide with a long thin corolla tube. Fruit is a woody capsule.

Bloom Season: Spring and early summer

Habitat/Range: Dry hills and rocky slopes from low to mid elevations on the east side of the Cascades.

Comments: *Oenothera* ("wine-scented") refers to the use of the powdered roots in winemaking. *Caespitosa* ("low-growing") refers to the low stature of the plant. Sphinx moths are a primary pollinator of these flowers that bloom in the evening. There are several varieties of this plant in the Northwest.

PALE EVENING PRIMROSE
Oenothera pallida
Evening Primrose Family (Onagraceae)

Description: Perennial. Reddish stems, smooth or hairy, arise erect or low growing, 4–28" long. Leaves are lance shaped to linear, 1–2½" long. White flowers consist of 4 petals, numerous stamens and a 4-lobed stigma. Fruit is a long, narrow capsule.

Bloom Season: Early to midsummer

Habitat/Range: Dry sandy or gravelly areas east of the Cascades from Washington to Arizona and east to Idaho and New Mexico.

Comments: *Oenothera* ("wine-scented") refers to the use of the powdered roots in winemaking. *Pallida* ("pale") refers to the petal color. Individual flowers open in the afternoon and bloom for about a day, then fade to a pinkish color. Wildlife, like pronghorn, eat the blossoms.

RATTLESNAKE PLANTAIN
Goodyera oblongifolia
Orchid Family (Orchidaceae)

Description: Perennial with dark green oval or narrowly elliptical leaves that are mottled or have white stripes down the center. From the dark basal leaves, arises a stout flowering stalk, 10–16" high, covered with sticky hairs. Numerous small, dull white to greenish flowers, mostly arranged on one side of the stem, are borne at the tip. The petals and a sepal form a hood over the lip. Fruit is a capsule.

Bloom Season: Mid to late summer

Habitat/Range: Shady coniferous forests, from lowlands to higher elevations, and in moist or dry humus throughout much of western North America.

Comments: *Goodyera* is for John Goodyear (1592–1664), an English botanist. *Oblongifolia* ("oblong-shaped leaves") refers to the leaf shape. The common name is a reference to the snakeskinlike markings on the leaves; hence, the plant's herbal use in treating rattlesnake bites.

WHITE BOG-ORCHID
Platanthera dilatata
Orchid Family (Orchidaceae)

Description: Perennial, up to 30" tall and bearing leaves along entire stem. Leaves are oblong to lance shaped and are smaller towards the top of the stem. The small flowers are white to pale greenish, very fragrant, and arranged in a dense, candlelike cluster. The upper sepals and 2 petals form a hood, while the lower 2 sepals spread outwards. The lower petal forms a lip that narrows at the tip. Behind this lip is a slender nectar tube called the spur. Fruit is a many-seeded, egg-shaped capsule.

Bloom Season: Summer

Habitat/Range: Swamps, bogs, meadows, stream edges, and marshes at mid to subalpine elevations throughout the region and into the East and Southwest.

Comments: Because the flower stem twists, the upper flower petal appears to be the lower one. *Platanthera* ("broad anther") describes the anther, and *dilatata* ("spread out") refers to the lower sepals. Native Americans in British Columbia would wash themselves with this sweet-scented flower. Moths with long proboscises reach the nectar deep in the flower's spurs.

LADIES' TRESSES
Spiranthes romanzoffiana
Orchid Family (Orchidaceae)

Description: From fleshy roots arise 2–5 basal leaves that are straplike and up to 10" long. The flowering stalk, which averages 2–6" tall, bears numerous creamy to greenish white flowers arranged in distinct longitudinal rows. Individual flowers have sticky, hairy sepals and petals that form a hood, with the lower petal sharply bent downwards. Fruit is a capsule.

Bloom Season: Mid to late summer

Habitat/Range: Low to mid elevations in dry to moist meadows, streamsides, bogs, and woodlands across the region.

Comments: *Spiranthes* is from the Greek *speira* ("coil") and *anthos* ("flower") in reference to the twisted or braided appearance of the flowers. *Romanzoffiana* honors Count Romanzoff (Nikolei Rumliantzev, 1754–1826), a Russian who sent Kotzebue to explore Alaska.

OREGON OXALIS
Oxalis oregana
Wood-Sorrel Family (Oxalidaceae)

Description: Perennial, ground cover. Flower and leaf stems arise from root nodes. Leaf stems are hairy, 2–8" tall, bearing shamrocklike leaves made up of 3 heart-shaped leaflets. Flowering stalks generally are shorter than the leaf stalks and bear a single white or pink funnel-shaped flower. The 1"-wide flowers have red or purple veins on the 5 petals. Fruit is a football-shaped capsule.

Bloom Season: Spring

Habitat/Range: Grows in shady woods at low to mid elevations from Washington to northern California on both sides of the Cascades.

Comments: *Oxalis* is from the Greek *oxys* ("acid") referring to the sour flavor of the leaves that contain oxalic acid. *Oregana* ("of Oregon") refers to the type locality. Also called Redwood Sorrel. This plant may form a dense understory, and the leaves fold up at night or during rainstorms.

TALUS COLLOMIA
Collomia larsenii
Phlox Family (Polemoniaceae)

Description: Perennial, matlike growth up to 1'
wide. Grayish leaves are highly divided and
covered with fine hairs. The ¾" wide tubular
flowers are white to pink or lavender and have 5
lobes with light purple lines. Fruit is a seed.

Bloom Season: Late summer

Habitat/Range: Scree and talus slopes at
subalpine to alpine elevations in Washington to
California and east to Wyoming and Utah.

Comments: *Collomia* is from the Greek *kolla*
("glue"), which refers to the seeds becoming
sticky when wet. The tiny stature is protection
against the alpine elements for these short-lived
perennials.

GRANITE GILIA
Leptodactylon pungens
Phlox Family (Polemoniaceae)

Description: Perennial, matlike growth up to 20"
long. The ¼–½" long, needlelike leaves form
dense clusters along the stems. The leaves are
divided into 3–7 segments, similar to fingers on a
hand. Flowers are funnel-shaped and white, and
have 5 flaring petals that may be tinged with
pink. In bud the 1"-long flowers are twisted shut.
Fruit is a tiny seed.

Bloom Season: Spring to midsummer

Habitat/Range: Rocky or sandy areas in dry areas
from low to mid elevations east of the Cascades
and into Idaho.

Comments: *Leptodactylon* ("narrow fingers")
refers to the spiny leaves that are divided into
fingerlike segments. *Pungens* ("sharp-pointed")
describes the tips of the leaves. The flowers
unfurl at night and attract moths with nectar. Also
called Prickly Phlox.

HOOD'S PHLOX
Phlox hoodii
Phlox Family (Polemoniaceae)

Description: Perennial, cushionlike growth. Leaves are spiny and ¼" long. White, 5–petaled flowers barely rise above the leaves. The flowers are ½" wide and have a yellow center. Fruit is a capsule.

Bloom Season: Spring

Habitat/Range: Dry areas in grassland, sagebrush flats, and open woodlands from low to mid elevations east of the Cascades.

Comments: *Phlox* ("flame") refers to the color of some species. *Hoodii* is possibly for Lieutenant Robert Hood of Britain's Franklin expedition to the Arctic in the early 1820s.

ALPINE BUCKWHEAT
Eriogonum pyrolifolium
Buckwheat Family (Polygonaceae)

Description: Perennial, low-growing with reddish stems up to 7". The oval-shaped basal leaves are ½–1½" long, borne on stalks, and smooth above and hairy below. The small flat-topped clusters of white, greenish white, or pinkish rose flowers arise from a 3–4" stem with reddish hairs. Two leaflike bracts sit below the flower clusters. The turban-shaped flowers have petal-like sepals that are less than ¼" long and have white to rose-colored hairs. The flowers also have an unpleasant odor. Fruit is a 3-angled seed.

Bloom Season: Late summer

Habitat/Range: Rocky outcrops, pumice, and sandy ridges at subalpine and alpine elevations in the Cascades from Washington to California and east to the Rocky Mountains.

Comments: *Eriogonum* ("woolly knees") refers to the hairs growing at the stem and leaf joints. *Pyrolifolium* ("pyrola-like leaves") refers to the leaf's similarity to those in the *Pyrola* genus. Also called Dirty Socks after the floral aroma; this odor attracts numerous pollinators including small butterflies and flies.

BEACH KNOTWEED
Polygonum paronychia
Buckwheat Family (Polygonaceae)

Description: Perennial, sprawling plant with upright or horizontal woody stems. The leaves have sheathing, paperlike bases where they attach to the stem. The elliptical leaves are 1" long and tough with margins that roll under the edge. The flowers are borne in clusters at the branch tips; the white to pink flowers are less than ¼" long and have 8 stamens. Fruit is a black seed.

Bloom Season: Summer

Habitat/Range: Coastal sand dunes and beaches from Vancouver Island to southern California.

Comments: *Polygonum* ("many knees") refers to the many joints along the stems. *Paronychia* refers to a "whitlow" or infection near a finger or toenail, for which a poultice of Beach Knotweed was applied. This knotweed colonizes sand dunes and may grow with Beach Morning Glory *(Convolvulus soldanella)* with its pinkish purple funnel-shaped flowers. Also called Black Knotweed after the black seeds.

AMERICAN BISTORT
Polygonum bistortoides
Buckwheat Family (Polygonaceae)

Description: Perennial with 1 to several unbranched stems, 10–35" tall, arising from a central base. Stems bear a few long-stalked, lance-shaped, or elliptical leaves along the lower stem. Leaves are 7–10" long, while the upper leaves are smaller and stalkless. Small white to pinkish flowers are borne in dense clusters, 1–3" long. Fruits are small, 3-angled yellowish brown seeds

Bloom Season: Summer

Habitat/Range: Wet meadows or streambanks at higher elevations across the western United States and Canada.

Comments: *Polygonum* ("many knees") refers to the jointed stems, while *bistortoides* ("twice twisted") refers to the plant's thick, twisted root and earns the plant the nickname Snakeroot. Native Americans roasted or boiled the roots for food. Lewis and Clark collected the first specimen of this plant in 1806.

PUSSYPAWS
Calyptridium umbellatum
Purslane Family (Portulacaceae)

Description: Perennial (at higher elevations and sometimes annual at lower), with 2–10" flowering stems radiating outwards and sprawling over the ground. Club- to spatula-shaped leaves, ½–2" long are arranged in a basal pattern and are smooth and shiny. Reddish flowering stalks extend from the leaves and bear a round cluster of fuzzy white to pink flowers. Each ¼"-flower has 2 round and papery sepals that surround the 4 smaller petals and stamens. The petals wither before the sepals. Fruit is a seed.

Bloom Season: Late spring into summer

Habitat/Range: Dry, sandy, pumice or gravelly sites at mid to alpine elevations across the region and into Utah.

Comments: *Calyptridium* ("having a calyptra") for the caplike covering of the flower. *Umbellatum* ("flowers in an umbel") describes the arrangement of the flowers in an umbrella-like pattern. During the day, the stems may elevate the flowers protecting the leaves from overheating and perhaps making the flowers more attractive to pollinators. The common name is after the clusters of flowers resembling a cat's upturned paw.

WESTERN SPRING BEAUTY
Claytonia sibirica
Purslane Family (Portulaceae)

Description: Annual, plants 2–16" tall. Basal leaves are fleshy, have long stems and elliptical to strap-shaped blades that are pointed. The small ¼–¾" flowers are white to pink and have a notch at the tip. Fruit is a capsule.

Bloom Season: Early spring to fall

Habitat/Range: Widespread at sea level to mid elevations from Siberia to Alaska and south to California.

Comments: *Claytonia* is for John Clayton (1685–1773), an American botanist who collected plants in Virginia. *Sibirica* ("Siberia") represents a portion of its distribution. The leaves are edible.

BITTERROOT
Lewisia rediviva
Purslane Family (Portulacaceae)

Description: Low-growing perennial arising from a fleshy, carrot-shaped root. Basal leaves are fleshy and rounded and often wither before the flowers mature. Upper stem leaves are very small and bractlike. White to rose-colored flowers are showy, 1–3" wide and made up of 12–18 petals. The fruit is a capsule.

Bloom Season: Mid spring to midsummer

Habitat/Range: Gravelly, rocky or sandy soils from sagebrush plains to low elevation woodlands from British Columbia to California and east to Montana and Colorado.

Comments: Named for Meriwether Lewis (1774–1809), expedition co-leader of the Corps of Discovery. *Rediviva* ("brought back to life") refers to the dried root's ability to sprout, as one of Lewis's collected specimens was able to sprout in President Jefferson's garden. Northwest tribes collected the prized roots in spring and boiled them before eating. Bitterroot is the state flower of Montana. The flowers open up by midday and attract a variety of pollinators.

WESTERN STARFLOWER
Trientalis borealis
Primrose Family (Primulaceae)

Description: Perennial, low-growing mostly 4–8" high but may be up to 15" tall. Egg-shaped leaves, 1–4" long, are arranged in whorls around the stem. From 3–8 leaves occur just below the flowers; lacks other stem leaves. The ½"-wide white to pink flowers have 4–9 (mostly 6–7) pointed petals, and are borne on slender stalks with 1–4 flowers in a cluster. Fruit is a rounded capsule.

Bloom Season: Late spring to midsummer

Habitat/Range: Meadow edges, roadsides, and shaded woods in low to mid elevations from British Columbia south to central California, and also in northeastern Washington and northern Idaho.

Comments: *Trientalis* ("one-third of a foot") refers to the height of this plant. *Borealis* ("boreal") refers to the plant's northern distribution. The common name is after the star-shaped arrangement of the petals. Northern Starflower *(T. arctica),* which also grows in the Northwest, has white flowers and several stem leaves below the upper whorl of leaves, and grows in wetland habitats.

BANEBERRY
Actaea rubra
Buttercup Family (Ranunculaceae)

Description: Perennial, grows up to 3' tall. Plants bear few leaves, generally one near the base and others higher on the stem. Leaves are divided 2 or 3 times into divisions bearing 3 leaflets (ternately compound). Leaflets are sharply toothed and lobed. Terminal rounded cluster of tiny white flowers with protruding stamens resembles an elongated white ball. Fruits are mostly reddish (white also) smooth berries.

Bloom Season: Spring to early summer

Habitat/Range: Moist, shady locations from sea level to subalpine elevations across most of the Northwest and temperate North America.

Comments: Baneberry is from the Anglo-Saxon word *bana* ("murderous") and refers to the highly toxic compounds in the berries, roots, and leaves. *Actaea* is from the Greek word *aktea* ("elder") referring to the similarity of Baneberry leaves to those of Elderberry. *Rubra* ("red") defines the primary color of the berries. Plants contain berbine and other toxic compounds.

WINDFLOWER
Anemone deltoidea
Buttercup Family (Ranunculaceae)

Description: Perennial, 6–15" tall. Basal leaves divided into 3 segments, while stems leaves are a whorl of 3 broadly lance-shaped leaves, with toothed margins, that are 1–2" long. White flowers are up to 1½" wide and have 5 white sepals and numerous stamens arising from a green center. The fruit is a seed with long hairs.

Bloom Season: Mid spring to early summer

Habitat/Range: Grows in moist or shady sites from low to subalpine forests, west of the Cascades (except the Olympic Mountains) to northern California.

Comments: The derivation of *Anemone* is unclear. *Deltoidea* ("triangular") refers to the triangular pattern of the stem leaves. Western Pasqueflower *(A. occidentalis)* and Pasqueflower *(A. patens)* are 2 showy windflowers with highly dissected leaves. Plants produce greater quantities of pollen than nectar to attract pollinators.

ALPINE WHITE MARSH-MARIGOLD
Caltha leptosepala
Buttercup Family (Ranunculaceae)

Description: Perennial, stems smooth and fleshy, growing 4–16". Basal leaves are oval to oblong, longer than broad, and somewhat arrowhead-shaped at the base. The white or greenish flowers, borne 1–2 per stem, are 1–2" wide. The outside of the flower is often tinged with blue. Fruit is a dry follicle that splits open when the seeds are mature.

Bloom Season: Summer

Habitat/Range: Wet mountain meadows (meadows, seeps, streambanks) at higher elevations in the subalpine and alpine regions from Alaska to Colorado and east to central Idaho.

Comments: *Caltha* ("cup or goblet") describes the shape of the flower, and *leptosepala* ("with slender sepals") describes the sepals. Native Alaskan peoples ate the leaves and flower buds, as well as the plant's slender, white roots. Elk browse on the leaves that contain toxic alkaloids without harm; hence, Cowslip and Elk's Lip are two other common names for the plant. Broad-Leaved Marsh-Marigold *(C. biflora)* is similar but has wider kidney-shaped leaves. Beetles are a common pollinator of these flowers.

WHITE VIRGIN'S BOWER
Clematis ligusticifolia
Buttercup Family (Ranunculaceae)

Description: Perennial vine. Stems climb on vegetation or trail along the ground and may reach 10–40' long. The opposite leaves are compound with 5–7 egg-shaped leaflets that are lobed and toothed along the margin. The loosely arranged flowering cluster bears numerous white flowers, ½" wide, that are composed of 4 petal-like sepals and numerous stamens. Male and female flowers are borne separately on the same plant. The fruit is a seed with a long feathery tail.

Bloom Season: Mid spring to summer

Habitat/Range: Streambanks and canyon bottoms at low to mid elevations from British Columbia to California and east to the Rocky Mountains.

Comments: *Clematis* is a Greek name for different climbing plants. *Ligusticifolia* ("with leaves like *Ligusticum*") refers to the leaves resembling those of lovage.

FALSE BUGBANE
Trautvetteria carolinensis
Buttercup Family (Ranunculaceae)

Description: Perennial, up to 1–3' tall. Large maple-like leaves, 2–15" wide, are lobed like a hand with 5–11 lobes. The lobes are toothed along the margin. Upper leaves smaller. The flattish flower heads are borne on long stalks; the 1"-wide white flowers lack petals and have numerous (50–70) white stamens. The sepals fall off as the flower matures. Fruit is a papery seed with a hooked tip.

Bloom Season: Late spring and summer

Habitat/Range: Moist, open woods and along streams and waterways from low to mid elevations throughout the western United States and British Columbia.

Comments: *Trautvetteria* is for Ernst Rudolf von Trautvetter (1809–1889), a Russian botanist associated with the St. Petersburg botanical garden. *Carolinensis* ("of North or South Carolina") refers to an eastern variety collected in 1788. The plants have protoanemonin, an alkaloid, that causes blistering or redness to the skin. Tall Bugbane *(Cimifuga elata)* is similar but taller and with larger leaves and flowers in a narrow, elongated cluster. The hooked seeds disperse by attaching to passing mammals.

SNOWBRUSH
Ceanothus velutinus
Buckthorn Family (Rhamnaceae)

Description: Perennial, shrub 3–8' tall. Evergreen leaves are egg shaped and glossy above and hairy below. A sticky varnish covers the leaves. The tiny white flowers grow in thick cluster; individual flowers have 5 petals that narrow at the base. Fruit is a seed.

Bloom Season: Midsummer

Habitat/Range: Dry hillsides and forests at low to mid elevations from British Columbia to California.

Comments: *Ceanothus* is the Greek name for a related spiny shrub. *Velutinous* ("velvety") refers to the leaf texture. Bees pollinate the aromatic flowers; the abundant blooms seem to "hum" due to the numerous bees attracted to the flowers. It's also an important winter browse plant for deer and elk. This is a fire-adapted species with seeds that need fire to germinate.

SERVICEBERRY
Amelanchier alnifolia
Rose Family (Rosaceae)

Description: Shrub, generally 3–15' tall but reaches 30'. Bark is gray to reddish. The deciduous leaves are round to oval and toothed along the upper margin. Five-petaled flowers are white, ½–1½" wide, and grow in small clusters. Narrow petals surround a dense cluster of yellow stamens. Fruit is a pome (applelike) that changes color from red to purplish black at maturity.

Bloom Season: Spring to summer

Habitat/Range: Widespread in meadows, forest edges, rocky slopes, and dry to moist open forests from low to mid elevations throughout western North America.

Comments: *Amelanchier* is from the archaic French *amelancier* that refers to another individual of this genus. *Alnifolia* ("alderlike leaves") refers to the resemblance of these leaves to those of the alder. Native Americans collected the edible fruits and mixed them with buffalo or venison to form pemmican. Deer, elk, and rabbits browse on the twigs and leaves. Leaves turn yellow in the fall.

GOAT'S BEARD
Aruncus dioicus
Rose Family (Rosaceae)

Description: Perennial, with hairless stems 3–6'
tall. Lower leaves 3 times compound, large and
with pointed leaflets with a pointed tip. Upper
leaves smaller and 1–2 times compound. The tiny,
white flowers are borne in long plumes of male
and female flowers on separate plants. Fruit is a
narrow pod.

Bloom Season: Early to midsummer

Habitat/Range: Edges of forests, roadsides, or
streams at low to mid elevations from Alaska to
California and eastward from British Columbia to
Idaho, also found in Eurasia.

Comments: *Aruncus* is from the Greek *aryngos*
("a goat's beard") and refers to the flower
plumes' resemblance to the hairs on a goat's chin.
Dioicus ("two homes") refers to the male and
female flowers borne on separate plants.
Northwest tribes used the plants to cure blood
diseases, as a diuretic, to treat smallpox, to treat
sore throats, and as a poultice for bruises and
swelling.

FERN-BUSH
Chamaebatiaria millifolium
Rose Family (Rosaceae)

Description: Shrub, 3–6' tall with spreading
stems covered with sticky and star-shaped hairs.
Fernlike leaves, 1–2½" long, are highly divided
several times. Flower clusters are 2–10" long and
bear ½" wide white, bell-shaped flowers with
numerous stamens. Fruit is a several-seeded
narrow pod.

Bloom Season: Early to midsummer

Habitat/Range: Drier sites in desert canyons or
mountain slopes at mid elevations east of the
Cascades from central Oregon to southern
California and east to Idaho.

Comments: *Chamaebatiaria* is from the Greek
Chamaibatos ("a dwarf bramble") and refers to
the low, sprawling nature of this shrub.
Millifolium ("with 1,000 leaves") refers to the
numerous small leaflets.

COASTAL STRAWBERRY
Fragaria chiloensis
Rose Family (Rosaceae)

Description: Perennial, with long runners. The stiff, leathery compound leaves are made up of 3 leaflets that are toothed along the margin. The upper sides of the leaves have prominent veins and the lower sides have silky white hairs. The white flowers are 1–2" wide with 5–7 petals and numerous stamens. Fruit is a small red berry about ¾–1" wide.

Bloom Season: Spring through summer

Habitat/Range: Coastal sand dunes and rocky outcrops at low elevations from Alaska to central California, but also in Hawaii and the coast of South America.

Comments: *Fragaria* is the Roman name for strawberries. *Chiloensis* ("of Chile") refers to the South American distribution of this plant. Rodents, birds, and humans consume the edible fruits. Numerous species of flies and bees are attracted to the flowers, although the plants can spread and root by aboveground runners. This plant does well in a cultivated, coastal garden.

BROADPETAL STRAWBERRY
Fragaria virginiana
Rose Family (Rosaceae)

Description: Perennial, low-growing with runners. Bluish green leaves are elliptical to oblong and toothed along the margins. The terminal tooth is smaller than the ones to its side. The white flowers are 1" wide and have 5 petals and numerous stamens. Fruit is a red berry.

Bloom Season: Mid spring to midsummer

Habitat/Range: Open woods, meadows, streambanks, and grasslands from low to mid-elevations mostly on the east side of the Cascades from Alaska to California and east to the Atlantic coast.

Comments: *Fragaria* is the Roman name for strawberries *Virginiana* ("of Virginia") refers to the location of the first collected specimen. The small edible berries are very sweet. Woodland Strawberry *(F. vesca)* also occurs in the region.

OCEANSPRAY
Holodiscus discolor
Rose Family (Rosaceae)

Description: Shrub, up to 15' tall. Stems are reddish brown with prominent ribs. The oval leaves are 1–3" long, have shallow lobes, and are hairy below and toothed along the margins. White flowers are borne in dense clusters. Fruit is a flat seed.

Bloom Season: Summer

Habitat/Range: Open areas in woodlands or rocky slopes from coastal to subalpine elevations from British Columbia to California and east to Montana.

Comments: *Holodiscus* is from the Greek *holos* ("entire") and *diskos* ("a disc") in reference to the unlobed saucer-shaped floral disk. *Discolor* ("of 2 different colors") refers to the white flowers that fade to tan when mature.

PARTRIDGEFOOT
Luetkea pectinata
Rose Family (Rosaceae)

Description: Small mat-forming perennial; plants 2–7" high. The densely clustered basal leaves are finely divided and fan-shaped. Stems leaves may be absent. Upright flowering stems bear dense clusters of tiny white to cream-colored flowers. Fruit is a small capsule that splits open at maturity.

Bloom Season: Summer

Habitat/Range: Prefers moist or shady sites in meadows or rocky sites from mid to alpine elevations in the northern mountains of western North America.

Comments: *Luetkea* honors Count F.P. Luetke (1797–1882), a Russian explorer and sea captain. *Pectinata* ("like the teeth of a comb") describes the finely divided leaf. The common name refers to the outline of the leaf that resembles the track of a partridge or ptarmigan. Also called Alaska Spirea.

TRAILING BLACKBERRY
Rubus ursinus
Rose Family (Rosaceae)

Description: Perennial with sprawling, prickle-bearing stems that may reach 15' long or upright stems to 50" tall. The deciduous leaves are compound with 3 deeply lobed leaflets that are toothed along the margin. The tip leaflet is dark green and 3 lobed. The white to pink, 5-petaled flowers have numerous stamens and may be up to 2" wide. Male and female flowers are borne on separate plants. Fruit is an edible berry.

Bloom Season: Late spring and midsummer

Habitat/Range: Widespread throughout the region west of the Cascades and into California in disturbed areas, open woodlands, thickets, and urban areas from low to mid elevations. This is the only native blackberry in the Northwest.

Comments: *Rubus* is the Latin name for blackberries, raspberries, and brambles. *Ursinus* ("like a bear") may refer to the color of the berry or the shape of the prickle resembling a bear's claw. The common Himalayan Blackberry *(R. discolor)* was introduced into the Northwest from Asia via England and is now naturalized in disturbed areas. The fragrant flowers attract bees, flies, wasps, and butterflies.

THIMBLEBERRY
Rubus parviflorus
Rose Family (Rosaceae)

Description: Shrub, generally 2–6' tall. Stems lack spines. Leaves 3–8" long and broad, covered with soft hairs, lobed like a maple leaf, and finely toothed along the margin. White flowers are 1–2" wide, with 5 wrinkled, papery petals and numerous yellow stamens. Fruit is a thimble-shaped red berry, resembling a raspberry.

Bloom Season: Mid spring to early summer

Habitat/Range: Widespread. Forests from low to high elevations from Alaska to Mexico and east to the Great Lakes region. Thimbleberries may colonize disturbed sites along roads, clearcuts, or burned areas.

Comments: *Rubus* is the Latin name for blackberries, raspberries, or brambles. *Parviflorus* ("with small flowers") refers to the size of the flowers. The thimble shape of the edible fruits gives its common name to this plant, which Lewis and Clark first collected along the Columbia River on April 15, 1806. A notation on their herbarium specimen written by Frederick Pursh reads: "A Shrub of which the natives eat the young Sprout without kooking." Black-tailed deer also browse the young leaves and stems, while birds and bears eat the fruits.

BASTARD TOAD-FLAX
Comandra umbellata
Sandalwood Family (Santalaceae)

Description: Perennial, often spreading by lateral roots. Plants are up to 13" tall. Erect stems bear linear, lance-shaped or narrowly elliptical leaves that are ⅜–1¼" long. Flowers are arranged in a flat-topped cluster. They lack petals, but have 5 whitish green sepals. Fruit is a 1-seeded nut covered with a purplish or brown fleshy coating.

Bloom Season: Spring

Habitat/Range: Sandy soils in grasslands or sagebrush habitat across much of the semi-arid western United States.

Comments: *Comandra* is from the Greek *kome* ("hair") and *andros* ("man"); the stamens (male reproductive parts) are hairy at the base. *Umbellata* ("umbel-like") refers to the flat-topped floral clusters. Bastard Toad-Flax is known to be parasitic on over 200 plant species although it can survive without a host. Rootlike connections called haustoria attach to a host's roots and pirate water and nutrients from those roots.

SMALL-FLOWERED ALUMROOT
Heuchera micrantha
Saxifrage Family (Saxifragaceae)

Description: Perennial up to 3' tall with dense white to brownish hairs on leaf stems and lower portion of flowering stalk. Leaf blades longer than broad with rounded, shallow lobes. Flowers borne in open clusters, the individual white flowers are very small. Fruit is a many-seeded capsule; seeds are covered with rows of tiny spines.

Bloom Season: Mid to late spring

Habitat/Range: Moist areas along streambanks or slopes or rocky outcrops from low to subalpine elevations from British Columbia to California and east to western Idaho.

Comments: *Heuchera* honors Johann Heinrich von Heucher (1677–1747), professor of medicine in Wittenberg, Germany. *Micrantha* ("small-flowered") refers to the tiny flowers. Smooth Alumroot *(H. glabra),* which has wider than longer leaves and hairless stems, is similar. Native coastal people made a poultice from the pounded root that was applied to cuts.

SMALL-FLOWERED STARFLOWER
Lithophragma parviflora
Saxifrage Family (Saxifragaceae)

Description: Perennial, reddish stems up to 14" long. The basal leaves are deeply lobed and round and have long stems. The flowering stalk leaves are smaller with narrow segments. The ⅜"-wide flowers are white to pink and deeply 3-lobed. Fruit is a small capsule.

Bloom Season: Spring

Habitat/Range: Open grasslands or sagebrush flats from British Columbia to California and east to the Dakotas.

Comments: *Lithophragma* is from the Greek *lithos* ("stone") and *phragma* ("wall") describing one habitat where this genus grows. *Parviflora* ("small flowers") refers to the size of the flowers. Several other species exist in the region; all have lobed flowers.

FRINGED GRASS-OF-PARNASSUS
Parnassia fimbriata
Saxifrage Family (Saxifragaceae)

Description: Perennial, with flowering stems 6–20" high. The basal leaves are kidney-shaped, glossy, and borne on long stems. The leafless flowering stalks bear a solitary, 1"-wide flower with 5 fringed petals. The petals have green or yellow veins and the lower portion of the petal has hairs along the fringe. The flowers produce 5 fertile stamens alternating with sterile stamens that are divided into fingerlike lobes. Fruit is a capsule.

Bloom Season: Summer

Habitat/Range: Wet meadows, bogs, stream edges, and moist sites in forests at mid to alpine elevations from Alaska to California and east to the Rocky Mountains.

Comments: *Parnassia* is from a 16th-century name for an unrelated plant growing on Mount Parnassus in Greece, but refers to its high elevation preference. *Fimbriata* ("with a small fringe") describes the petals. Flies and mosquitoes pollinate these flowers as they obtain nectar from the exposed aromatic glands. Northern Grass-of-Parnassus *(P. palustris)* also occurs in the region but lacks the petal fringe.

NORTHWESTERN SAXIFRAGE
Saxifraga integrifolia
Saxifrage Family (Saxifragaceae)

Description: Perennial, often 4–8" but may reach 16" tall. Reddish stems may be hairy. Basal leaves reddish and densely hairy below, variable in shape and fringed with fine hairs on edges. Flowers are borne in small clusters at the tip of a long stem and the individual flowers have white or greenish petals and are ¹⁄₁₆–¼" up to ¼" wide. Seeds have small ridges.

Bloom Season: Early spring

Habitat/Range: Moist or dry grassy areas, streambanks, and subalpine meadows from low to mid elevations in British Columbia to California and east to central Idaho.

Comments: *Saxifraga* is from the Latin *saxum* ("a rock") and *frango* ("to break"). *Integrifolia* ("entire leaves") refers to the smooth leaf edge. More than 20 species of saxifrage occur in the Pacific Northwest. Blooms early in the spring and often in profusion.

WESTERN SAXIFRAGE
Saxifraga occidentalis
Saxifrage Family (Saxifragaceae)

Description: Perennial, 3–15" tall. Basal leaves are 1–3" long, leathery, egg shaped, and toothed along the margin. Single, flowering stems bear clusters of small white flowers that arise on reddish, woolly stems. Ten orangish stamens arise from the flowers. Fruit is a tiny seed.

Bloom Season: Spring

Habitat/Range: Moist meadows, grassy openings, and rocky slopes or outcrops from mid to subalpine elevations from British Columbia to Oregon and east to Idaho and northwest Wyoming, but mainly east of the Cascades.

Comments: *Saxifraga* is from the Latin *saxum* ("a rock") and *frango* ("to break") and refers to the rocky habitats these plants occur in and their supposed ability to break apart rocks. *Occidentalis* ("western") refers to the plant's Northwest distribution.

TOLMIE'S SAXIFRAGE
Saxifraga tolmiei
Saxifrage Family (Saxifragaceae)

Description: Perennial, forming dense mats up to 24" wide. The basal leaves are fleshy, linear, and up to ½" long, and form dense mats. The red, flowering stalks are 2–4" tall and bear ⅜"-wide white, star-shaped flowers. Located between the 5 white, paddle-like petals, are white petal-like rods that contain stamens with black anthers. The greenish center contains the stigma and ovaries. Fruit is an oval capsule that has purplish mottling.

Bloom Season: Summer

Habitat/Range: Rocky outcrops, cliff faces or bare moist soil mostly in subalpine or alpine areas from Alaska to central California and east into central Idaho.

Comments: *Saxifraga* is from the Latin *saxum* ("a rock") and *frango* ("to break") and refers to the rocky habitats these plants occur in and their supposed ability to break apart rocks. *Tolmiei* is for William Fraser Tolmie (1812–1886), a Scottish physician for the Hudson Bay Company stationed at Fort Vancouver in the early 1830s who collected plants in the Northwest. Tolmie Peak near Mount Rainier is named after him.

FRINGECUP
Tellima grandiflora
Saxifrage Family (Saxifragaceae)

Description: Perennial, 1– 3½' tall. Basal leaves are heart shaped and 2–4" wide with 5–7 shallow lobes that are toothed. The few stem leaves are similar but smaller. Tubular bell-shaped flowers have 10 stamens and are borne along in loose clusters on a long stalk. Petals are frilled and greenish white or pink but turn dark red with age. Fruit is a capsule.

Bloom Season: Late spring to midsummer

Habitat/Range: Moist woods, streambanks, and up to lower elevation mountain slopes from southern Alaska to California on west side of the Cascades, but also in Columbia River Gorge and into northern Idaho.

Comments: *Tellima* is an anagram of *Mitella,* another genus in the Saxifrage Family. *Grandiflora* ("large-flowered") refers to the sizeable flowers.

FOAMFLOWER
Tiarella trifoliata
Saxifrage Family (Saxifragaceae)

Description: Perennial, from creeping underground stems (rhizomes). Upright stems clustered or single and 6–20" tall. Basal leaves either 3-lobed, divided into segments, or with 3 leaflets. Leaves are coarsely hairy and up to 6" wide. Upper leaves smaller. Small white flowers, ⅛" long, are borne in a loose cluster above the leaves. The narrow petals resemble the stamen stems. Fruit is a few-seeded capsule.

Bloom Season: Summer

Habitat/Range: Forms a low ground cover in moist woodlands from low to subalpine elevations from Alaska to California and east to Montana.

Comments: *Tiarella* is from the Greek *tiara* ("ancient Persian headdress"), which the fruit resembles. *Trifoliata* ("3 leaves") refers to the divided leaves. The common name refers to the flower color resembling specks of foam. The large leaves collect filtered sunlight that penetrates to the forest floor in the dense woodlands. Bees and other pollinators clasp the flowers in search of nectar or pollen, often bending the entire flowering stalk under their weight.

SICKLETOP LOUSEWORT
Pedicularis racemosa
Figwort Family (Scrophulariaceae)

Description: Upright perennial that may grow to 2' tall. Upper lance-shaped leaves are larger than lower ones and have short stalks. Leaf edges are doubly saw-toothed. Flowers are whitish but mostly pink to purplish. Flower's upper lip tapers into a sickle-shaped, curved beak, while petals in larger lower lip spread outwards. Fruit is a flat, curved capsule.

Bloom Season: Summer

Habitat/Range: Coniferous woods at mid to subalpine elevations throughout the region and across much of the West.

Comments: *Pedicularis* ("pertaining to lice") refers to the idea that grazing livestock became infected with lice when foraging in fields with members of this genus. The common name describes the sickle-shaped flowers. *Racemosa,* refers to the arrangement of the stalked flowers along an unbranched stem (a raceme), where the flowers mature from the base upwards.

SCABLAND PENSTEMON
Penstemon deustus
Figwort Family (Scrophulariaceae)

Description: Perennial to 16" tall. The woody stems branch at the base and tend to form dense clumps of flowering stalks. The variable shaped leaves are mostly toothed along the margin and lance- or inversely lance-shaped. The upper leaves lack petioles and are much smaller than the lower leaves. Long flowering stalks bear a dense cluster of white or creamy (occasionally yellow), 2-lipped flowers. The upper lip is shorter than the lower lip and often appears shriveled; the lower petals have purplish nectar guidelines near the throat. Fruit is a small capsule.

Bloom Season: Early summer

Habitat/Range: Dry and rocky outcrops or cliffs from low to subalpine elevations from central Washington to southern California and east to northern Utah.

Comments: *Penstemon* is from *pen* ("almost") and *stemon* ("stamen"), which refers to the sterile stamen called a staminoide typical of this genus. *Deustus* ("scorched or burned up") refers to the color of the upper petals. The sterile stamen is hairless or sparsely hairy at the tip.

INDIAN TOBACCO
Nicotiana attenuata
Potato Family (Solanaceae)

Description: Annual. Plants 1–4' tall, with sticky hairs on stems and leaves. Leaves are elliptical to broadly lance-shaped. White flowers are trumpet- or funnel-shaped and 1–2" long, and the lobes on the calyx are shorter than the calyx tube. The stamens are borne on either long or short stalks. Fruit is a capsule that contains numerous tiny black seeds.

Bloom Season: Mid to late summer

Habitat/Range: Dry sandy sites at low to mid elevations east of the Cascades.

Comments: *Nicotiana* honors Jean Nicot de Villemain (1530–1600), the French ambassador to Portugal who is credited with introducing tobacco plants into France in the 16th century. *Attenuata* ("pointed") refers to the sepal tips. Moths pollinate the deep, tubular flowers.

SITKA VALERIAN
Valeriana sitchensis
Valerian Family (Valerianaceae)

Description: Perennial. Square stems range from 1–3' (up to 5') tall and are mostly smooth and somewhat succulent. Two or more pairs of leaves arise oppositely at points along the flowering stem. The compound leaves have 3–7 oval or lance-shaped leaflets, with the end leaflet being the largest. Leaf margins are coarsely toothed. Tiny white to pinkish flowers are arranged in 1–3" wide flat-topped or hemispherical clusters at the top of the plant. The stamens arise above the 5-petaled, fragrant flowers. The fruit is a seed with feathery hairs on the top.

Bloom Season: Late spring to early summer

Habitat/Range: Widespread from mid to subalpine elevations in moist meadows, streambanks, moist forested slopes, and subalpine forests from Alaska to Montana and south to California.

Comments: *Valerian* is probably derived from the Latin word *valere* ("to be healthy or strong") and refers to the plant's medicinal qualities. *Sitchensis* ("of Sitka") refers to location of the first collected species. The roots have a strong aroma that is a sharp contrast to the sweet-smelling flowers. Northwest tribes used the pounded roots as a poultice for cuts and wounds.

YELLOW FLOWERS

This section includes flowers that range
from pale to bright yellow. Check the
white, green, red, or orange sections
if you don't find your plant here.

GRAY'S DESERT PARSLEY
Lomatium grayi
Carrot Family (Apiaceae)

Description: Perennial, clump-forming. Compound leaves divided into numerous, dark green, narrow segments. The yellow flowers are arranged in dense, flat-topped clusters that arise on leafless stems. Fruit is a flattened seed.

Bloom Season: Spring

Habitat/Range: Rocky outcrops and talus slopes in dry grasslands or sagebrush flats along east side of Cascades from central Washington to northern Idaho.

Comments: *Lomatium* is from the Greek *loma* ("a border or edge") and refers to the dorsal ribs or "wings" that adorn the seeds. *Grayi* honors the American botanist Asa Gray (1810–1888), a Harvard professor who wrote *Gray's Manual of Botany* in 1848. When crushed, the leaves have a strong odor. The flat-topped clusters attract numerous insects as pollinators.

LARGE-FRUITED LOMATIUM
Lomatium macrocarpum
Carrot Family (Apiaceae)

Description: Perennial, from a thick taproot. Compound leaves are highly dissected (3 times), are covered with hairs and have purple undersides. Flowering stalks bear flat-topped clusters of yellow or white flowers that may be tinged with purple. Fruits are large, ½–¾" seeds.

Bloom Season: Spring

Habitat/Range: Dry open plains or rocky areas east of the Cascades from British Columbia to California.

Comments: *Lomatium* is from the Greek *loma* ("a border or edge") and refers to the dorsal ribs or "wings" that adorn the seeds. *Macrocarpum* ("large seed") refers to the size of the seed.

MARTINDALE'S LOMATIUM
Lomatium martindalei
Carrot Family (Apiaceae)

Description: Perennial, from a deep taproot with low-growing stems 2–10" tall. Basal blue-green leaves are highly dissected and toothed or lobed along the margin. The terminal leaf segments are deeply divided. Flat-topped clusters of tiny yellow to yellowish white flowers are 1–2" wide. Fruit is a flattened seed with corky ribs and papery wings.

Bloom Season: Late spring and summer

Habitat/Range: Dry sites on rocky outcrops, talus or scree slopes, or meadows at mid to alpine elevations from southern British Columbia to southern Oregon.

Comments: *Lomatium* is from the Greek *loma* ("a border or edge") and refers to the dorsal ribs or "wings" that adorn the seeds. *Martindalei* is for Isaac Martindale (1842–1893), an American who amassed a large private herbarium in the 19th century. The large root system stores nutrients and moisture to enable the plant to survive through long winters or drought. Also called Few-Fruited Lomatium.

NINE-LEAF BISCUITROOT
Lomatium triternatum
Carrot Family (Apiaceae)

Description: Perennial, 1–2' tall. Compound leaves dissected into 3 segments that are further divided into narrow, linear segments that are ½–5" long. Flowers borne in small clusters combine to form larger flat-topped clusters. Fruit is a flattened seed with papery wings and ribs.

Bloom Season: Late spring into early summer

Habitat/Range: Moist to dry sites meadows and open slopes at low to mid elevations from British Columbia to California and east to Utah.

Comments: *Lomatium* is from the Greek *loma* ("a border or edge") and refers to the dorsal ribs or "wings" that adorn the seeds. *Triternatum* ("triply ternate") describes the highly divided leaves. This plant has several varieties and subspecies.

SKUNK CABBAGE
Lysichitum americanum
Arum Family (Araceae)

Description: Perennial, which grows 1–2½' tall. Huge broadly lance-shaped or elliptical leaves grow in a basal rosette around a stout stem; the leaves may be 1–4½' long and half as wide. A bright yellow hood partially surrounds the greenish yellow flowering stalk (called a spadix) that bears numerous tiny greenish yellow flowers. The berrylike fruits are embedded in the flowering stalk.

Bloom Season: Early to late spring

Habitat/Range: Wet areas like swamps, bogs, moist forest areas, or fens at mid to lower elevations from Alaska to central California and east to Idaho.

Comments: *Lysichitum* is from the Greek *lysis* ("releasing") and *chiton* ("a cloak") and refers to the yellow hood that falls apart with age. *Americanum* ("from America") refers to the distribution of this North American species. Though the plant contains oxalate crystals that cause irritation and burning to the mouth and throat, Pacific Northwest natives ate the leaves, roasted or steamed, but only during desperate times. Legend has it that Skunk Cabbage kept the native people alive before the salmon arrived. To honor the plant, they gave an elk-skin blanket and war club to the plant and set it in rich, moist soil near a river. Bears eat the roots and deer will forage on the leaves. Pollinators include beetles, bees, and flies, and slugs will "pirate" the pollen.

HEART-LEAVED ARNICA
Arnica cordifolia
Sunflower Family (Asteraceae)

Description: Perennial. The basal, heart-shaped leaves with toothed margins arise from the stem in an opposite arrangement. The upper leaves are broadly lance-shaped and toothed on the margins. The long flowering stalk (6–20") arises above the leaves and bears a single yellow head. The 2–3" wide flower head has both ray and disk flowers; the rays have shallow notched tips. Fruit is a seed with white hairs.

Bloom Season: Early to midsummer

Habitat/Range: Widespread in moist, open woods in low to subalpine elevations across the region from Alaska to California often on the east side of the Cascades.

Comments: *Arnica* is from the Greek word *arnakis* ("lambskin") and refers to either the woolly bracts that subtend the flower heads or the leaves' hairy undersides. *Cordifolia* ("heart leaf") refers to the leaf shape. Arnicas are unique in this family due to the opposite leaves. Poultices and tinctures made from the dried leaves were, and still are, used as a disinfectant and to treat muscle strains and bruises.

RAYLESS ARNICA
Arnica discoidea
Sunflower Family (Asteraceae)

Description: Perennial. Plants arise from lateral roots just below the ground surface. Lower leaves are opposite, egg to nearly heart shaped, and arising on long stalks. The margins are irregularly toothed and the blades are 2–4" long. Upper leaves are smaller and lack a stalk. The flower heads are ½–¾" wide , have numerous yellow disk flowers, and lack ray flowers; the young heads do not hang downwards. Fruit is a seed with white hairs.

Bloom Season: Summer

Habitat/Range: Open woods at mid elevations along the Cascades from Washington to California.

Comments: *Arnica* is from the Greek word *arnakis* ("lambskin"), which refers to either the woolly bracts that subtend the flower heads or the hairy undersides of some leaves. *Discoidea* ("without rays") refers to the rayless flower heads.

WESTERN MUGWORT
Artemisia ludoviciana
Sunflower Family (Asteraceae)

Description: Perennial, upright stems, 12–40"
tall. Stem leaves are 1–3" long, linear to lance
shaped and grayish woolly on the upper surface
and with white hairs on the underside. The lower
leaves are variable and may be entire or lobed.
The flowering heads are borne in a loose cluster;
the small heads bear yellow disk flowers. Fruit is
a smooth seed that lacks hairs.

Bloom Season: Late summer and fall

Habitat/Range: Dry and open sites from low to
subalpine elevations throughout North America
and into Mexico.

Comments: *Artemisia* commemorates Artemis,
the Greek goddess of chastity. *Ludoviciana* ("of
Louisiana") refers to the Louisiana Territory where
Meriwether Lewis collected this plant in 1806 on
his return journey to St. Louis. The crushed leaves
are very fragrant. Big Sagebrush *(A. tridentata)* is
a widespread shrub with 3-lobed leaves.

ARROWLEAF BALSAMROOT
Balsamorhiza sagittata
Sunflower Family (Asteraceae)

Description: Perennials that grow ½–2' tall and
as wide or wider. Arrow-shaped leaves may be
10" long and 6" wide and are smooth along the
margin. The stout flowering stalk bears a 2–4"
wide flower head with large yellow ray and disk
flowers. Fruit is a seed.

Bloom Season: Late spring to early summer

Habitat/Range: Drier areas from sagebrush plains
to mid elevation forests throughout the east side
of the region.

Comments: *Balsamorhiza* ("balsam root") refers
to the balsamlike aroma of the roots. *Sagittata*
("arrow-shaped") refers to the leaf shape. True
sunflowers *(Helianthus)* have leaves along the
flowering stalk, whereas balsamroots do not bear
leaves on their flowering stems. Native
Americans harvested the young shoots and roots
of the plant in spring as food or medicine, and
collected the oily seeds in summer. Deer and elk
browse on the leaves. Deltoid Balsamroot *(B.
deltoidea)* has triangular leaves that lack hairy
undersides.

SILVERCROWN
Cacaliopsis nardosmia
Sunflower Family (Asteraceae)

Description: Perennial, with stout stems 2–4' tall. Roundish basal leaves have long stems, are 8–10" wide and resemble a deeply lobed maple leaf. Upper leaves fewer and smaller. Yellow flowers are borne in a dense cluster; the flower heads are ½–1½" wide. Individual tubular disk flowers have paired stigmas that protrude above the flowers. Fruit is a seed with numerous white bristles.

Bloom Season: Early to midsummer

Habitat/Range: Open woods and meadows at mid to high elevations along the east side of the Cascades from Washington to Oregon.

Comments: *Cacaliopsis* ("*Cacalia*-like") is a reference to the similarity of this genus to *Cacalia*. *Nardosmia* ("spikenard smell") refers to the flowers having a fragrant aroma. Tongue-Leaf Luina *(C. stricta)* has pale yellow flowers, and the plants occur in subalpine meadows in the Cascades.

COLUMBIA TICKSEED
Coreopsis tinctoria
Sunflower Family (Asteraceae)

Description: Annual or biennial with stems 1–4' tall. The compound leaves have many linear leaflets. The flowering heads, 1–2" wide, have yellowish ray flowers with a reddish brown base surrounding a center of brownish disk flowers. Fruit is a black, winged seed often with 2 dark projections.

Bloom Season: Midsummer to fall

Habitat/Range: Moist sites along streams at low elevations from Washington to Oregon and east to Idaho.

Comments: *Coreopsis* is from the Greek *koris* ("a bug") and *opsis,* indicating a resemblance in reference to the ticklike seed. *Tinctoria* ("used in dyeing") refers to the yellowish orange dye made from the flowers.

SPRING-GOLD
Crocidium multicaule
Sunflower Family (Asteraceae)

Description: Annuals, 3–6" tall, and often multistemmed. The basal leaves are slightly fleshy and inversely lance-shaped, while the stem leaves are smaller. Woolly hairs grow between the leaf and the stem, and they often persist as the plant matures. Flower heads bear both yellow ray and disk flowers and are about ½" wide. Seed has thick hairs that become sticky when wet.

Bloom Season: Early spring

Habitat/Range: Dry, open fields, cliff edges, and sandy plains at low elevations from Vancouver Island to California.

Comments: *Crocidium* is derived from the Greek word *krose* or *krokys* ("wool or loose thread") and refers to the hairs growing in the leaf axils. *Multicaule* ("many stems") describes the form, although there may be only a single stem. Also called Gold Stars. Though individuals are small, large patches of these flowers may blanket the ground in early spring.

RUBBER RABBITBRUSH
Ericameria nauseosus
Sunflower Family (Asteraceae)

Description: Shrub, 2–6' tall, with stems covered with dense hairs. Leaves are alternate and linear. Yellow flowers are borne in dense clusters of 5–20 disk flowers, the clusters often cloaking the plant. Fruit is a seed with fine hairs.

Bloom Season: Late summer to fall

Habitat/Range: Dry sites in sagebrush or open coniferous forests from low to mid elevations in southern British Columbia to California and east through Idaho.

Comments: *Ericameria* is from the Greek *erica* ("heath") and *meris* ("division or part") in reference to the heathlike leaves. *Nauseosus* ("nauseating") refers to the plant's strong scent. Native Americans harvested the flowers in the late summer or fall for use as a yellow dye. Green Rabbitbrush *(E. viscidiflorus)* has smooth twigs and leaves that are usually twisted and slightly sticky. Flowers pollinated by butterflies, flies, beetles, bees, and wasps.

LINE-LEAVED FLEABANE
Erigeron linearis
Sunflower Family (Asteraceae)

Description: Perennial, 2–12" tall with a cushionlike growth. The basal leaves are linear and 1–4" long. Flower heads are borne singularly and bear 20 or more yellow ray flowers that surround a center of yellowish orange disk flowers. The flower-head bracts have short hairs. Fruit is a seed with a tuft of small white hairs.

Bloom Season: Late spring and early summer

Habitat/Range: Dry or rocky sites in sagebrush flats or forests up to mid elevations in the mountains from British Columbia to Oregon on the east side of the Cascades.

Comments: *Erigeron* is from the Greek *eri* ("early") and *geron* ("old man") referring to the white hairs on the seeds. *Linearis* ("linear") refers to the narrow, pencil-thin leaves.

OREGON SUNSHINE
Eriophyllum lanatum
Sunflower Family (Asteraceae)

Description: Perennial with multiple stems forming either low-growing mats or upright clumps. Stems, leaves, and flower-head bracts are covered with dense, white hairs. Leaves are variable from paddle shaped to linear, opposite (or alternate), and have 3–7 lobes at the tip. A single flower head (1–2" wide) is borne on a long stalk and bears 7–15 yellow ray flowers that are about ¾" long. The ray flowers surround a cluster of darker yellow disk flowers. Fruit is a smooth seed.

Bloom Season: Late spring to fall

Habitat/Range: Dry sites, meadows, rocky slopes from sea level to subalpine areas mostly on eastern side of the Cascades from British Columbia to California and east to Montana.

Comments: *Eriophyllum* ("woolly leaf") and *lanatum* ("woolly") refer to the "woolly" nature of the stem, leaves, and leaflike bracts that surround the flower heads. Another common name is Woolly Sunflower. Plants attract a wide variety of pollinators over their long blooming season.

BROWN-EYED SUSAN
Gaillardia aristata
Sunflower Family (Asteraceae)

Description: Perennial, up to 3' tall. Leaves long-stemmed, up to 5" long, inversely lance-shaped, and lobed or toothed along the margin. Flower heads, 1–3" wide, are borne on long stalks and bear up to a dozen deeply notched ray flowers surrounding a center of reddish brown disk flowers. The wedge-shaped ray flowers are 1" long, 3-lobed at the tip, and may have a purplish base. Fruit is a seed topped with stiff bristles.

Bloom Season: Summer

Habitat/Range: Dry or moist sites in meadows, plains, and roadsides from mid elevations in southern British Columbia to northern Oregon on the east side of the Cascades.

Comments: *Gaillardia* honors Gaillard de Charentonneau, an 18th-century French magistrate and botanical patron. *Aristata* ("bearded") refers to the hairs that cover the receptacle. Also known as Blanket Flower or Black-Eyed Susan, this plant does well in cultivated gardens.

SLENDER CUDWEED
Gnaphalium canescens
Sunflower Family (Asteraceae)

Description: Perennial, up to 2' tall. The stems and leaves are covered with dense hairs. Narrow leaves are 1–5" long. The flowering heads are borne in broad clusters; each head is comprised of tiny yellow to white disk flowers. Fruit is a seed with hairy bristles.

Bloom Season: Midsummer to fall

Habitat/Range: Open areas, often in disturbed or burned sites, throughout the region.

Comments: *Gnaphalium* is from the Greek *gnaphalion*, (a downy plant with soft leaves). *Canescens* ("hairy") refers to the dense hairs on the plant.

PUGET SOUND GUMWEED
Grindelia integrifolia
Sunflower Family (Asteraceae)

Description: Many branched perennial that grows from 7–40". Long, lance-shaped basal leaves and shorter, stalkless stem leaves have sticky glands. Flower heads are ½–2" wide and bear yellow ray flowers surrounding a center of yellow disk flowers. Sticky, resin-coated green bracts subtend the flowers. Seeds have multiple awns that fall off.

Bloom Season: Summer

Habitat/Range: Mostly maritime, found at beaches, rocky shorelines, salt marshes, and in low elevation nonmaritime moist locations from Washington to Oregon.

Comments: Named after David Grindel (1776–1836), a Russian botanist. *Integrifolia* ("entire-leaved") refers to the smooth margins of the upper leaves, not the lower toothed ones. Idaho Gumweed *(G. nana)* occurs on the drier, eastern side of the Cascades.

SNEEZEWEED
Helenium autumnale
Sunflower Family (Asteraceae)

Description: Perennial, with angled stems, 7–48" tall. The numerous lance-shaped leaves are alternate and lack a stem. The flowering heads are somewhat spherical with yellow disk flowers surrounded by 10–20 yellow, 3-lobed ray flowers that project downwards. The heads are ½–1½" wide. Fruit is a seed with pointed scales.

Bloom Season: Late summer to fall

Habitat/Range: Widespread in moist locations at low elevations throughout the region.

Comments: *Helenium* is from *helenion,* a different plant named for Helen of Troy. *Autumnale* ("pertaining to autumn") refers to the blooming period of the flowers—late summer to fall. The flowers and green buds make a yellow dye. The flowers attract a variety of pollinators, including butterflies.

HAIRY GOLDENASTER
Heterotheca villosa
Sunflower Family (Asteraceae)

Description: Perennial, generally sprawling but may grow erect to 20". Lower leaves wither before the flowers open, but the upper strap-shaped leaves do not. The yellow flower heads are about 1" wide and have 10–25 ray flowers that encircle numerous yellow disk flowers. The hairy bracts that subtend the flowering head are overlapping. Fruit is a seed.

Bloom Season: Summer

Habitat/Range: Dry, sandy ground or rocky sites from southern British Columbia throughout the Pacific Northwest.

Comments: *Heterotheca* is from *heteros* ("different") and *theke* ("ovary") for the different seeds that form from the ray and disk flowers. *Villosa* ("soft haired") describes the fine hairs on the leaves and stems; hence, the common name—hairy.

DWARF HULSEA
Hulsea nana
Sunflower Family (Asteraceae)

Description: Low-growing perennial. Leaves mostly basal, hairy, and inversely lance-shaped with shallow lobes. Flower stalks bear a single, bell-shaped flower head with numerous yellow ray and disk flowers. The bracts that subtend the flower heads are numerous and in 2 or 3 rows. Fruit is a seed with stiff hairs.

Bloom Season: Mid to late summer

Habitat/Range: Subalpine to alpine elevation on cinder cones, pumice soils, and meadows from Mount Rainer to Northern California.

Comments: *Hulsea* honors Dr. Gilbert White Hulse (1807–1883), a US Army surgeon and botanist. *Nana* ("dwarf") refers to the plant's low stature. These fragrant plants may bloom in profusion and attract late season butterflies, bees, wasps, and flies.

ROUGH CAT'S EAR
Hypochaeris radicata
Sunflower Family (Asteraceae)

Description: Perennial, stems 6–30" tall. The basal leaves are variable, with toothed edges and stiff hairs. The branched stems are smooth and bear flowering heads comprised of yellow ray flowers that are about 4 times as long as wide. The heads are ½–1½" wide and open in sunny or cloudy weather. Fruit is a seed with a long parachute of white hairs.

Bloom Season: Summer

Habitat/Range: Introduced from Europe, this weedy species occurs in disturbed areas, from sea level to mid elevations throughout the region, but mainly west of the Cascades and northern Idaho.

Comments: *Hypochaeris* is a name used by ancient Greeks for this or a related plant. *Radicata* ("with rooting stems") refers to the perennial nature of the plant. Cat's Ear resembles the common dandelion *(Taraxacum officinale).*

FALSE AGOSERIS
Nothocaulis troximoides
Sunflower Family (Asteraceae)

Description: Perennial, low growing. Basal leaves are long and narrow and have waxy or crisped margins. A solitary yellow flower head is borne at the end of a leafless stem and bears only ray flowers. The bracts below the flower clusters are more or less lance-shaped and may have dark spots. Fruit is a club-shaped seed with numerous white hairs at the tip.

Bloom Season: Spring and early summer

Habitat/Range: Dry, open sites in the lowlands and foothills of the mountains from eastern Washington to Montana and south to Utah.

Comments: *Nothocaulis* is from the Greek *nothos* ("false") and *caulis* ("stem") referring to the leafless stalk that resembles a stem.

SILVER RAILLARDELLA
Raillardella argentea
Sunflower Family (Asteraceae)

Description: Perennial, low growing. Basal leaves are 1–2½" long, grayish green because of the numerous fine hairs. The flowering stalks are ½–6" long and bear a single flowering head of yellow disk flowers. The bracts below the flowering head are almost equal in length and end with a pointed tip. The fruit is a flattened seed with stiff hairs at the tip.

Bloom Season: Mid to late summer

Habitat/Range: Open woodlands or bare ground in subalpine to alpine areas from central Oregon to northern California.

Comments: *Raillardella* (similar to *Raillardia*) indicates this plant's similarity to that genus. *Argentea* ("silvery") refers to the coloration of the leaves. The plant may spread by underground roots creating dense mats. Small butterflies and other insects are attracted to the plants for their nectar or pollen.

WOOLLY SENECIO
Senecio canus
Sunflower Family (Asteraceae)

Description: Perennial, plants 6–18" tall with hairy stems. Basal leaves appear silvery due to numerous white hairs, are lance to egg shaped, and are 1–2" long. The stem leaves are smaller and few. Flower heads are arranged in loose flat-topped clusters; the heads have 5–8 (up to 13) yellow ray flowers surrounding a yellowish center of disk flowers. The bracts below the flowering heads have black tips. The fruit is a ribbed seed with white hairs.

Bloom Season: Early summer

Habitat/Range: Dry, open sites east of the Cascades at low to subalpine elevations along the east side of the Cascades.

Comments: *Senecio* is from the Latin *senex* ("old man") and refers to the white hairs atop the seeds. *Canus* ("off-white") refers to the silvery appearance of the leaves.

TANSY RAGWORT
Senecio jacobaea
Sunflower Family (Asteraceae)

Description: Biennial, stems 1–6' tall. The stout stems bear numerous fernlike leaves, 2–5" long, that are highly dissected and with toothed lobes. The upper leaves are smaller. The numerous flowering heads form a dense cluster at the top of the plant. Individual heads have 10–15 ray flowers surrounding a center of disk flowers. Fruit is a seed with numerous white hairs.

Bloom Season: Summer

Habitat/Range: Introduced from Europe, this plant is found throughout North America in disturbed sites.

Comments: *Senecio* is from the Latin *senex* ("old man") and refers to the white hairs atop the seeds. *Jacobaea* honors St. James (Jacobus), whose saint's day is July 25 and coincides with the late summer blooming period of this weed. The plants contain a toxin that discourages wild or domestic herbivores and enables the plant to spread. Numerous types of pollinators, from bees to wasps to butterflies, are attracted to these flowers. Also called Stinking Willie. Arrow-Leaved Butterweed *(S. trianugularis)* has toothed, triangular leaves.

CANADA GOLDENROD
Solidago canadensis
Sunflower Family (Asteraceae)

Description: Perennial, stems 2–6' tall. The lance-shaped to elliptical stem leaves lack a petiole and are entire to toothed along the margin, smooth or hairy, and 2–7" long. The lower leaves fall off before flowering. The dense flowering heads are arranged in a pyramid-like cluster. The heads have leaflike, pointed bracts below and 10–20 tiny yellow ray flowers. Fruit is a small seed with white hairs.

Bloom Season: Midsummer to fall

Habitat/Range: Fields, thickets, meadows, forest or streambanks, and disturbed areas at low to mid elevations throughout the western United States.

Comments: *Solidago* is from *solidus* ("whole") and ago ("to make") in reference to the medicinal properties of goldenrod. *Canadensis* ("of Canada") refers to its type locality. The flowers attract bees, wasps, and butterflies as pollinators. Giant Goldenrod *(S. gigantea)* has smooth stems with a whitish coating.

SEASIDE TANSY
Tanacetum camphoratum
Sunflower Family (Asteraceae)

Description: Perennial, often growing on sandy hummocks. Stout stems, 1–24" tall, bear fernlike leaves that are highly divided and have long, white hairs on the undersides. The ¼–¾" wide flower heads are button-shaped with numerous yellow disk flowers. Fruit is a ribbed seed.

Bloom Season: Summer

Habitat/Range: Coastal sand dunes and beaches from British Columbia to northern California.

Comments: *Tanacetum* is from the Latin *tanazita* ("immortality"). *Camphoratum* ("camphorlike") refers to the plant's resemblance to camphor. Early settlers added the crushed leaves to burial sheets to discourage worms. Brass Buttons *(Cotula coronopifolia)* also has yellow buttonlike flowers but the leaves are oblong in shape and are not cleft, except for the lower leaves.

YELLOW SALSIFY
Tragopogon dubius
Sunflower Family (Asteraceae)

Description: Annual or biennial with a stout, 1–2' stem. Leaves are long and grasslike. Flower heads are 1½–3" wide, and have numerous lemon-yellow ray flowers with long and pointed flower-head bracts extending beyond the ray flowers. The seed heads are round, and the seeds are topped with stiff hairs.

Bloom Season: Summer

Habitat/Range: Widespread in disturbed sites throughout the region but more common east of the Cascades.

Comments: *Tragopogon* ("goat's beard") may refer to the silky hairs on the seeds resembling those of a goat's beard. *Dubius* ("doubtful") has an unclear meaning. The derivation of salsify translates to "sun follower" although the flowers may close during the day or on cloudy days. The roots, eaten raw or steamed, have a flavor similar to oysters; hence, another common name is Oyster Plant. Common Salsify *(T. porrifolius)* is similar but has a deep purple flowering head. Blooms in summer and attracts flies, bees, wasps, beetles, and butterflies as pollinators.

NORTHERN MULE'S EARS
Wyethia amplexicaulis
Sunflower Family (Asteraceae)

Description: Often growing in profusion, the plants may be 1–2' tall. Basal, lance-shaped leaves are 12–15" long and very glossy. Stem leaves are smaller. Yellow flowers have both ray and disk flowers and are 2–3" wide. Fruit is a seed.

Bloom Season: Late spring

Habitat/Range: Grows in open, meadows in mid to higher elevation areas.

Comments: *Wyethia* is for Nathaniel Wyeth (1802–1856), the "Cambridge Iceman" who led 2 expeditions to Oregon in 1832 and 1834. Wyeth was the first American to travel to the Northwest along the route that would later become the Oregon Trail. *Amplexicaulis* ("stem clasping") refers to the leaves, which lack petioles.

OREGON GRAPE
Berberis aquifolium
Barberry Family (Berberidaceae)

Description: Shrub, 2–4' tall. The hollylike compound leaves have 5–11 evergreen leaves that are saw toothed and spiny along the margin. Yellow flowers are borne in dense clusters. The petals are 2 lobed. The grapelike fruits are bluish.

Bloom Season: Spring

Habitat/Range: Both sides of the Cascades from British Columbia to Oregon and east to Idaho.

Comments: Originally placed in the genus *Mahonia,* named after Bernard McMahon, a Philadelphia nurseryman who grew the plants from seeds brought back East by Meriwether Lewis, the name changed to *Berberis. Aquifolium* ("shiny leaves") describes the leaf surface. Sometimes called Oregon Holly Grape after the hollylike leaves and grapelike fruits. This is the state flower of Oregon. The fruits make a blue dye and the roots a yellow one.

CASCADE OREGON GRAPE
Berberis nervosa
Barberry Family (Berberidaceae)

Description: Shrub, low-growing up to 2' tall. Compound leaves have 11–19 evergreen leaflets that have spiny margins. The broadly lance-shaped leaflets are up to 3" long. Flowers borne in a dense cluster that may be 8" long. Yellow flowers have similar sepals and petals that are arranged in whorls. The stamens are attached to the inner petals. Fruit is a blue to purple berry.

Bloom Season: Late spring to midsummer

Habitat/Range: Woodlands from low to mid elevations from British Columbia to central California.

Comments: *Berberis* originates from the Arabian name for the fruit. *Nervosa* ("conspicuous nerves") refers to the prominent leaf veins. When an insect lands in the center of the flower, the stamens collapse inwards and dust the insect with pollen. Native tribes (as well as wildlife) ate the fruits, and a yellow dye was made from the roots.

MENZIES' FIDDLENECK
Amsinckia menziesii
Borage Family (Boraginaceae)

Description: Annual, stems 7–35" tall. Stems, leaves, and flowers have stiff hairs. Linear leaves are ¾–1½" long. Small yellow-orange flowers arranged in a coiled or scorpion tail-like pattern. The fused petals form a flaring collar and a short tube. Fruit is a small nutlet.

Bloom Season: Spring

Habitat/Range: Grasslands and dry disturbed sites mostly east of the Cascades at low elevations.

Comments: *Amsinckia* honors Wilhelm Amsinck (1752–1831), a patron of the Botanical Garden in Hamburg, Germany. *Menziesii* honors Archibald Menzies (1754–1842), a Scottish physician and naturalist who accompanied Captain George Vancouver on his 1790–1795 Pacific exploration. The common name is after the coiled spike of flowers, which resembles a fiddle's neck.

WESTERN GROMWELL
Lithosperma ruderale
Borage Family (Boraginaceae)

Description: Perennial with clustered stems that may grow up to 30" tall. Leaves and stems are covered with short, stiff hairs. The leaves seem to crowd out the flowers. The small, funnel-shaped flowers are a pale yellow and ½" wide and flare open at the end. Fruit is a nutlet.

Bloom Season: Late spring to early summer

Habitat/Range: Dry grassland or forests from low to mid elevations from British Columbia to northern California and east to Colorado.

Comments: *Lithosperma* is from the Greek words *lithos* ("stone") and *sperma* ("seed") and refers to the smooth, stonelike seed. *Ruderale* ("growing in waste places") refers to habitat conditions where these plants occur. The fragrant flowers attract butterflies as pollinators.

ROUGH WALLFLOWER
Erysium capitatum
Mustard Family (Brassicaceae)

Description: Biennial, stout stems, 6–36" tall. Leaves linear, rough textured, up to 5" long, and covered with fine hairs. Flowers borne in dense terminal clusters are yellow and 4-petaled. Petals are ½" long and arranged in a cross pattern. Fruit is a slender pod, 1–4" long.

Bloom Season: Late spring to midsummer

Habitat/Range: Dry, sandy areas east of the Cascades at low to mid elevations from British Columbia to California and east to Texas.

Comments: *Erysium* is from the Greek *erysio* ("to draw") after a species that was used medicinally as a poultice to induce skin blisters and draw out pain. *Capitatum* ("dense head") refers to the flowers. Sand-Dwelling Wallflower *(E. arenicola)* is similar but with greener leaves and flattened pods. It occurs up to subalpine areas in the Cascades and Olympic Mountains.

PLAINS PRICKLY-PEAR
Opuntia polyacantha
Cactus Family (Cactaceae)

Description: Perennial, with jointed stems. Flattened stems are fleshy, straight spined, and variable in size. Showy flowers are 3–6" across with numerous yellow to red petals surrounding many stamens. Fruit is a spiny, many-seeded berry.

Bloom Season: Mid spring to early summer

Habitat/Range: Dry, open ground in grasslands, plains, and sagebrush flats from low to mid elevations throughout the drier portions of the region.

Comments: *Opuntia* is the Greek name for a different plant growing near the ancient Greek town of Opus. *Polyacantha* ("with many thorns") describes the stems. The green stems contain chlorophyll pigments necessary for photosynthesis. The edible fruits are sweet, and the stems were also eaten with the spines burned off. Several barrel-shaped cactus occur in the region as well.

YELLOW BEE PLANT
Cleome lutea
Caper Family (Capparidaceae)

Description: Annual, stems may reach 3' tall in optimal conditions. Compound leaves have generally 5 (3 to 7) elliptical leaflets that arise from a common point. The upper leaves are small and bractlike. Clusters of golden-yellow flowers arise at the end of the plant. The 6 stamens protrude beyond the 4 sepals and petals. Fruit is a pod that hangs downward and contains several roughened black seeds.

Bloom Season: Spring

Habitat/Range: Sandy soils in dry sites in sagebrush steppe and mountain valleys from eastern Washington to Montana and south to Utah.

Comments: The derivation of *Cleome* is uncertain. *Lutea* ("yellow") refers to the dye color made from the flowers. Golden Bee Plant *(C. platycarpa)* has similar flowers and leaves with 3 leaflets. It occurs in eastern Oregon and southern Idaho. Native Americans ate the leaves as a potherb.

BEARBERRY HONEYSUCKLE
Lonicera involucrata
Honeysuckle Family (Caprifoliaceae)

Description: Shrub, plants mostly 3–7' (up to 12') tall. Opposite leaves are elliptical and pointed at the tip. Yellow flowers are borne in pairs in leaf axils. The tube-shaped flowers are ½–1" long and have two sticky, leaflike bracts at their bases. These bracts change from green to red or purple with age. Fruit is a black, round berry.

Bloom Season: Spring

Habitat/Range: Moist woods, streambanks and clearings from sea level to subalpine elevations across much of western North America.

Comments: *Lonicera* honors Adam Lonitzer (1528–1586), a German herbalist. *Involucrata* ("with an involucre") refers to the conspicuous floral bracts. The bitter fruit has been reported as both edible and poisonous. The dark berries were used as a dye by some coastal tribes; hence, it is also called Ink-Berry, Twinberry or Bush Honeysuckle. Hummingbirds pollinate the flowers by day, and Hawk Moths pollinate the flowers at night.

SPREADING STONECROP
Sedum divergens
Stonecrop Family (Crassulaceae)

Description: Perennial, mat-forming with flowering stems 2–6" tall. The fleshy leaves are opposite, egg shaped, ⅛–½" wide, and are green to red in color. The flowering stalks bear clusters of yellow flowers that have long, pointed petals. The flowers are ¼–1" wide. Fruit is a pod.

Bloom Season: Summer

Habitat/Range: Rocky outcrops and talus slopes in coastal or subalpine to alpine elevations from southern British Columbia to Oregon.

Comments: *Sedum* is from the Latin *sedo* ("to sit") referring to the low-growing plants covering rocky outcrops or stone walls. *Divergens* ("spreading") refers to the outstretched petals. Also called Oregon Stonecrop. Broad-Leaved Stonecrop *(S. spathulifolium)* is similar but with larger, alternate leaves in basal rosettes.

AMERICAN PINESAP
Hypopitys monotropa
Heath Family (Ericaceae)

Description: Saprophyte, reddish stems 8–15" tall. The scalelike leaves lack chlorophyll. The yellowish brown, ½–1" long flowers are borne in dense clusters and the flowers hang downwards. Fruit is a capsule.

Bloom Season: Summer

Habitat/Range: Moist, forest humus from low to subalpine elevations throughout the region. Also occurs in Europe.

Comments: *Hypopitys* is from the Greek *hypo* ("under"), with *pitys* ("pine tree"), in reference to its habitat of growing below pine or coniferous trees. *Monotropa* ("one direction") refers to the flowers facing the same direction. The plant derives nutrients from soil fungi associated with their roots. Blooms turn black when mature.

PINEDROPS
Pterospora andromedea
Heath Family (Ericaceae)

Description: Perennial, 1 to several reddish brown stems arise 6–36". The scalelike leaves are reddish brown and basal. The top of the plant is a dense cluster of small, urn-shaped flowers that are yellowish brown and hang downward on short stalks. Fruit is a round capsule.

Bloom Season: Summer

Habitat/Range: Found east of the Cascades in dry pine woodlands, this plant ranges from Alaska to Mexico and east to the Rocky Mountains.

Comments: *Pterospora* ("winged seeds") describes the seeds, and *andromedea* ("Andromeda") is named after the mythical maiden chained to a rock and rescued by Perseus. Like other saprophytes, this plant derives its nutrients from fungi associated with its roots.

SCOTCH BROOM

Cytisus scoparius
Pea Family (Fabaceae)

Description: Shrub, may reach 10' tall and has green, angled stems. The compound leaves have 3 leaflets that are smooth along the edges. The bright yellow, pealike flowers are borne in a cluster of 2 to 3 along the majority of the stems. The flowers are up to 1" long. Fruit is a hairy pod that "pops" open.

Bloom Season: Spring and summer

Habitat/Range: Introduced from Europe, now widespread throughout the Northwest at low to mid elevations.

Comments: *Cytisus* is from the Greek *kytisos* a name applied to woody members of the Pea Family. *Scoparius* ("broomlike") refers to the stems, which could be collected and tied together making a broom. The plants were introduced to Vancouver, B.C., in the 1850s, and from there spread across the Northwest. Gorse *(Ulex europaea)* is a similar shrub with pea-shaped flowers introduced from Europe, but it has numerous spines. The sweet flowers attract numerous bees or bumblebees as pollinators.

NEVADA DEERVETCH

Lotus nevadensis
Pea Family (Fabaceae)

Description: Perennial, often with sprawling stems. Compound leaves borne on short stems, the 3–15 elliptical leaflets with glandlike appendages at the base of the stems. Flowers borne in small umbrella-like clusters from the leaf axils; the pealike, yellow flowers are tinged with red. Fruit is a small pod.

Bloom Season: Summer

Habitat/Range: Sandy or rocky sites in open woodlands or forest edges at mid elevations from British Columbia to California and east to Idaho.

Comments: *Lotus* is the Greek name for these plants. *Nevadensis* ("of Nevada") refers to the type locality. Bird's-Foot Trefoil *(L. corniculatus)* is a common, introduced relative widely distributed in the region—bees and butterflies pollinate both.

MOUNTAIN THERMOPSIS
Thermopsis gracilis
Pea Family (Fabaceae)

Description: Perennial, hollow stems arise 2–4'
and bear numerous compound leaves with 3
smooth leaflets. The upper part of the stem, the
sepals, and the pods are covered with silky hairs.
Yellow, pea-shaped flowers are borne in a dense,
elongated cluster. Flowers are about 1" long. Fruit
is a straight, upright pod.

Bloom Season: Late spring to early summer

Habitat/Range: Meadows and moist sites from
low to mid elevations from the Pacific Coast to
the Rocky Mountains.

Comments: *Thermopsis* ("resembling a lupine")
and *gracilis* ("graceful") refer to the lupinelike
flowers and slender stature. This plant is
unpalatable to livestock; therefore it may grow in
dense clusters. Bush Lupine *(Lupinus arboreus)* is
another yellow, pea-flowered plant that is
shrubby and occurs along the coast.

GOLDEN CORYDALIS
Corydalis aurea
Fumitory Family (Fumariaceae)

Description: Perennial but low-growing. Leaves
are highly divided into narrow segments. Yellow
flowers borne in small clusters; each flower is
narrow but bilaterally symmetrical and is made of
4 petals with a spur at the end. Fruit is a capsule.

Bloom Season: Summer

Habitat/Range: Grows in gravelly to sandy soils
in sagebrush flats or ponderosa pine woodlands
mainly east of the Cascades but throughout North
America.

Comments: *Corydalis* ("a lark") refers to floral
spur that resembles a lark's toe. *Aurea* ("golden")
refers to the flower color. Bees visit these flowers
to obtain nectar stored in the spur. Seedpods may
explode when mature, flinging seeds away from
the parent plant.

GOLDEN CURRANT
Ribes aureum
Currant Family (Grossulariaceae)

Description: Shrub, 2–10' tall with smooth stems. Leaves are 3-lobed, leathery and ¾–1½" long. The bright yellow flowers are borne in clusters of 5–18, are trumpet shaped with a long tube and 5 flaring lobes. Fruit is an orange, yellow, red, or black berry.

Bloom Season: Mid spring

Habitat/Range: Moist sites along streams, washes, and rivers from low to mid elevations, in grasslands up to ponderosa pine forests, east of the Cascades from British Columbia to California and east to the Rocky Mountains.

Comments: *Ribes* is derived from the Arabic *ribas* ("acid tasting") after the bitterness of the edible fruits. *Aureum* ("golden") refers to the flower color. Meriwether Lewis wrote that the yellow currants are: "transparent as the red current of our gardens, not so ascid, & more agreeably favored." The Northwest natives ate the berries, which are also consumed by birds.

YELLOW GLACIER LILY
Erythronium grandiflorum
Lily Family (Liliaceae)

Description: Perennial that grows 6–15" tall. The large, nonmottled basal leaves are arranged in pairs and clasp the flowering stem base. Atop the leafless flowering stem is a single (sometimes pairs) golden-yellow flower that hangs downward. The 6 tepals curve upwards, while the large yellow stamens protrude downwards. The 1"-long, club-shaped capsules contain papery seeds.

Bloom Season: Late spring to midsummer

Habitat/Range: Moist areas like meadows or avalanche paths at mid to alpine elevations from Washington to Oregon and east to the Rocky Mountains.

Comments: *Erythronium* is from the Greek *erthros* ("red") in reference to the pink or red flowers of some species. *Grandiflorum* ("large-flowered") refers to the flower's size. Plants may bloom near edges of snowfields or glaciers, hence, the common name. The plants are able to photosynthesize under the snow and often the leaves and buds push up through the snow. Native peoples harvested the edible root, which is also consumed by black bears. Small rodents, deer, elk, and bears eat the green seedpods. Avalanche Lily *(E. montanum)* is similar but has white flowers with yellow centers.

YELLOW BELL
Fritillaria pudica
Lily Family (Liliaceae)

Description: Perennial that grows 4–12" high from a small, white bulb. Stem bears 2–6 narrow, straplike leaves, ½–6" long. Flowering stalk bears 1–3 yellow, bell-shaped flowers that hang downwards. Flowers have 6 tepals. Fruit is a round or egg-shaped capsule.

Bloom Season: Early to late spring

Habitat/Range: Dry grasslands, woodlands, and open meadows at low elevations from British Columbia to California and east to Alberta.

Comments: *Fritillaria* is from the Latin *fritillus* ("a dice box"), which refers to the capsules. *Pudica* ("bashful") refers to the pendulous flowers. Lewis and Clark noted that the local Northwest tribes collected and ate the onionlike bulbs. Bees, flies, and beetles pollinate the flowers.

GREAT BLAZING STAR
Mentzelia laevicaulis
Blazing Star Family (Loasaceae)

Description: Perennial or biennial, plants up to 3'. Stems many branched and white. The basal leaves are lance shaped, up to 4" long, toothed along the margin, and rough textured. Upper leaves smaller. Starlike yellow flowers are 2–3" wide, with 5 pointed petals and a short, green bract between the petals. Numerous threadlike stamens project above the flower. Fruit is a capsule with tiny black seeds.

Bloom Season: Summer and early fall

Habitat/Range: Often in sandy or gravelly soils in dry sites at lower elevations east of the Cascades.

Comments: *Mentzelia* is for Christian Mentzel (1622–1701), a German botanist and physician. *Laevicaulis* ("smooth stem") describes the feel of the stem, as contrasting to the rough leaves. The flowers first open in the evening and then close in the morning until the petals mature; afterwards, the flowers remain open. Flies, beetles, moths, small bees, and wasps may be observed wandering through the "forest" of stamens in search of pollen. David Douglas first recorded this species along the Columbia River.

YELLOW SAND VERBENA
Abronia latifolia
Four-O'Clock Family (Nyctaginaceae)

Description: Low-growing perennial with prostrate stems up to 3' long. Stems have sticky hairs. Leaf blades are round to kidney or oval shaped, and are oppositely arranged along the stems. Flower heads contain several to many, tubular, ½"-long yellow flowers that flare open at the mouth. Fruits are cylindrical seeds adorned with thick, keel-like projections.

Bloom Season: Mid to late summer

Habitat/Range: Coastal sand dunes and beaches from British Columbia to northern California.

Comments: *Abronia* is from the Greek *abros* ("delicate or graceful"), which describes the bracts below the fragrant, slim flowers. *Latifolia* ("broad leaves") refers to the leaf shape. Sand grains adhere to the sticky hairs on the stems and leaves, hence the common name. Moths and hummingbirds use their long proboscises to probe the fragrant, tubular flowers for nectar. Shifting sands may bury portions of the plant, sometimes giving the appearance that the flowers are sprouting from the sand. Pink Sand Verbena (*A. umbellatum*) is similar but with pink flowers and a more southern range.

YELLOW POND-LILY
Nuphar lutea
Water-Lily Family (Nymphaeaceae)

Description: An aquatic perennial, the egg- to heart-shaped leaf blades are 6– 22" long and float on the water surface. Yellow flowers are 2" across and made of inconspicuous petals and small outer green sepals. The larger inner sepals are yellow but may have a purple or greenish tinge. Center of the flower is a large knoblike and long-stalked stigma. The fruit is an oval, ribbed capsule that releases seeds in a jellylike mass when mature.

Bloom Season: Late spring and summer

Habitat/Range: Ponds or standing water from low to mid elevations on both sides of the Cascades from Washington to California.

Comments: *Nuphar* is from the Arabic word *naufar,* a name for a water lily. *Lutea* ("yellow") refers to the flowers. Many Northwest tribes used the root for medicinal purposes and ate the seeds. Caddis flies are attracted to the flower's nectar, as are other flies and beetles. Also called Wokas or Wocus.

TANSY-LEAVED EVENING PRIMROSE
Camissonia tanacetifolia
Evening Primrose Family (Onagraceae)

Description: Perennial, lacks a stem and is low growing. Long leaves are highly lobed or divided; the leaves are 4" long. Yellow flowers, 1–2" wide, arise from a basal cluster of leaves and have 4 petals and long tubes. The 4 sepals turn backwards as the flower matures.

Bloom Season: Early summer

Habitat/Range: Grasslands, shrublands or meadows in pine woodlands that are seasonally moist. Generally at lower elevations east of the Cascades from Washington to northern California and east to Idaho and Montana.

Comments: *Camissonia* is for Adelbert Ludwig von Chamisso (1780–1838), a Russian botanist who collected plants in California in 1816. *Tanacetifolia* ("tansy-leaved") refers to the tansylike leaves. Beach Primrose *(C. cheiranthifolia)* is a low-growing relative that occurs in sand dunes and beaches along the coast, but with thick, non-lobed leaves.

HOOKER'S EVENING PRIMROSE
Oenothera elata
Evening Primrose Family (Onagraceae)

Description: Tall biennial that grows 1–5' tall. Leaves are lance shaped, smaller towards the top of the flowering stalk. The bright yellow flowers are 2–4" wide, with 4 slightly notched petals and 8 protruding stamens. The fruit is a capsule that splits open longitudinally when mature.

Bloom Season: Summer

Habitat/Range: Moist areas—streambanks, springs, open meadows, and disturbed sites throughout the region.

Comments: *Oenothera* ("wine-scented") refers to the roots being added to the process of wine making. *Elata* ("tall") refers to the plant's stature. The flowers open in the evening to attract Hawk Moths or Sphinx Moths as pollinators. Also called Giant Evening Primrose.

HEART-LEAVED BUCKWHEAT
Eriogonum compositum
Buckwheat Family (Polygonaceae)

Description: Perennial, clump forming. The basal leaves are 2–8" long, with arrow-shaped to triangular blades borne on long petioles and hairy undersides. The leafless flowering stems are 8–20" tall and support a compound, umbrella-like cluster of flowers with leaflike bracts below the umbels. Clusters are up to 4" wide. The smaller flowers are yellow or white and made up of sepals. Fruit is a seed.

Bloom Season: Mid spring to midsummer

Habitat/Range: Dry grasslands, rocky slopes, and cliffs at low to mid elevation from Washington to northern California and east to Idaho.

Comments: *Eriogonum* ("woolly knees") refers to the swollen joints on many of the species. *Compositum* ("compound") refers to the flowers. The flat-topped clusters attract butterflies, bees, and flies.

SULFUR-FLOWERED BUCKWHEAT
Eriogonum umbellatum
Buckwheat Family (Polygonaceae)

Description: The basal leaves of this perennial are egg- to spoon-shaped, arise on slim stalks, and are green above and gray-woolly below. From this basal cluster of leaves arise the flowering stems that vary from 2–20" tall; several leaflike, narrow bracts are arranged below the flower clusters. The numerous small, yellowish flowers that may be tinged with pink are clustered into umbrella-like forms. Individual flowers have 6 lobes and stamens that extend beyond the flower opening. Fruit is a 3-angled seed.

Bloom Season: Late spring and summer

Habitat/Range: Dry, rocky sites from mid to subalpine elevations from British Columbia to California and east to the Rocky Mountains.

Comments: *Eriogonum* ("woolly knees") refers to the swollen joints on many of the species. *Umbellatum* ("umbrella-like") refers to the inverted flower clusters, while the common name refers to the sulfur color of the flowers.

SMALL CREEPING BUTTERCUP
Ranunculus flammula
Buttercup Family (Ranunculaceae)

Description: Perennial, low growing up to 3" tall. Lateral stems trailing along the ground root at the leaf nodes, thus the flowering stems appear to be connected. The small leaves are linear and nonlobed. The ½" yellow flowers are borne on short stalks and have 5 shiny petals and numerous stamens. Fruit is a seed with a hooked beak.

Bloom Season: Summer

Habitat/Range: Grows in moist sites along the Northwest coast, but also found across Canada to the northeast United States.

Comments: *Ranunculus* is derived from the Latin *rana* ("frog") for the aquatic or moist habitat preference of the genus. *Flammula* ("a small flame") refers to the slightly bitter taste of the leaves. The open dishlike flower attracts numerous small flying insects. Creeping Buttercup *(R. repens)* is another species that can root at the leaf joints, but the basal leaves are divided into 3 lobed leaflets that may bear white dots.

SAGEBRUSH BUTTERCUP
Ranunculus glaberrimus
Buttercup Family (Ranunculaceae)

Description: Perennial, low-growing (2–6") from clustered roots. Basal leaves are fleshy and either broad with shallow lobes or divided into deeper lobes. The short flowering stalks bear 1" wide bright yellow flowers that have 4–7 petals and numerous stamens and pistils. Each petal has a nectar gland at the base. Fruit is a seed.

Bloom Season: Early to mid spring

Habitat/Range: Seasonally moist sites in sagebrush flats or pine woodlands at low to mid elevations from British Columbia to California and east to the Dakotas.

Comments: *Ranunculus* is derived from the Latin *rana* ("frog") for the aquatic or moist habitat preference of the genus. *Glaberrimus* ("without hairs") refers to the smooth leaves. Pollinators, such as beetles, flies, wasps, and other insects, visit the plentiful flowers for either nectar, located at the base of the petals, or pollen, which is produced in abundance by the stamens.

WESTERN BUTTERCUP
Ranunculus occidentalis
Buttercup Family (Ranunculaceae)

Description: Perennial, with 1 to many upright and spreading stems that are 7–30" tall. The long-stalked basal leaves have 3 wedged-shaped lobes with toothed divisions. Upper leaves smaller and more deeply divided. Several bright yellow flowers are borne at the end of long stalks. Flowers are ½–1" wide and the hairy sepals fall off as the flower matures. Fruit is a smooth seed with a hooked tip.

Bloom Season: Spring

Habitat/Range: Moist meadows, grassy areas, openings, and woodlands (open or shady) from coastal to subalpine elevations from Alaska to California.

Comments: *Ranunculus* is derived from the Latin *rana* ("frog") for the aquatic or moist habitat preference of the genus. *Occidentalis* ("western") describes the range of this plant. Flies, beetles, and other winged insects are attracted to the abundance of pollen produced by the flowers.

LARGE-LEAVED AVENS
Geum macrophyllum
Rose Family (Rosaceae)

Description: Perennial, with hairy stems up to 3' tall. Basal leaves with rough hairs are irregularly divided into small leaflets with a larger heart- to kidney-shaped leaflet at the tip. The stem leaves have 3 deep lobes or divisions. The ½"-wide, saucer-shaped yellow flowers have 5 rounded petals surrounding a center of numerous stamens. Fruit is a seed with hooked bristles.

Bloom Season: Late spring and midsummer

Habitat/Range: Open forests and edges from low to subalpine elevation from Alaska to Baja California and east to the Great Lakes.

Comments: *Geum* is the Latin name for the plant. *Macrophyllum* ("large-leaved") refers to the large basal leaves. Northwest tribes used the plant medicinally for eyewashes, stomach ailments, and child birthing. The seed's hooked bristles catch on the fur of passing animals to aid in seed dispersal.

PACIFIC SILVERWEED
Potentilla anserina
Rose Family (Rosaceae)

Description: Perennial, with sprawling stems and reddish runners. The compound leaves are divided into 9–31 leaflets that are toothed along the margin and have white hairs below. The leaves are 3–8" long. Bright yellow flowers, ¾–1½" wide are saucer shaped and borne singly. Fruit is a flattened, oval seed.

Bloom Season: Late spring to summer

Habitat/Range: Coastal beaches, headlands, swales, and open areas from Alaska to California.

Comments: *Potentilla* is from the Latin *potens* ("powerful") after the medicinal uses of the plant. *Anserina* ("related to geese") refers to the plants growing where geese forage. Coastal tribes ate the roots. The open flowers attract bees, flies, and butterflies as pollinators.

ANTELOPE BITTERBRUSH
Purshia tridentata
Rose Family (Rosaceae)

Description: Shrub, 2–6' tall. The wedge-shaped leaves are ½–1" long, hairy below and 3-lobed at the tip. The yellow flowers have 5 petals and numerous stamens and are ½–1" wide. Fruit is a seed.

Bloom Season: Spring

Habitat/Range: Drier sites in sagebrush or Ponderosa Pine forests at mid elevations from British Columbia to California and east to Colorado.

Comments: *Purshii* honors Frederick Traugott Pursh (1774–1820), a German botanist who worked on the Lewis and Clark plant collection and wrote *Flora Americae Septentrionalis,* a flora of North America, in 1814. *Tridentata* ("three-toothed") refers to the leaf tips. This is an important winter forage plant for wildlife.

COTTONY PAINTBRUSH
Castilleja arachnoidea
Figwort Family (Scrophulariaceae)

Description: Perennial, often with multiple stems 4–10". The leaves are hairy. Small greenish flowers are hairy and enclosed by reddish orange to greenish yellow bracts. Fruit is a capsule.

Bloom Season: Mid summer to fall

Habitat/Range: Dry sandy, gravelly or pumice soils at mid to alpine elevations in Oregon, California, and Nevada.

Comments: *Castilleja* is for Domingo Castillejo (1744–1793), a Spanish professor of botany. *Arachnoidea* ("resembling spider hairs") refers to the hairy leaves and bracts. Many Indian paintbrush species are difficult to distinguish from each other. Hummingbirds or butterflies pollinate most species of paintbrush.

YELLOW MONKEY-FLOWER
Mimulus guttatus
Figwort Family (Scrophulariaceae)

Description: An annual or perennial, this plant varies in size from 2–24" tall. The oval-shaped leaves grow in pairs; leaves may have hairs or smooth surfaces. Lower leaves are stalked and upper leaves clasp the stem. Borne on long stalks, the trumpet-shaped flowers are ¾–2" long, 2-lipped with one large or several smaller crimson spots on the lower lip. Fruit is a capsule.

Bloom Season: Late spring and summer

Habitat/Range: Moist sites from sea level to subalpine elevations throughout the region.

Comments: *Mimulus* is from *mimus* ("a mimic") referring to the flower resembling a monkey's face. *Guttatus* ("spotted") refers to the dots on the flower's lower lip. When an insect, like a bee, enters the flower, it contacts the stigma. The 2 lobes fold together and press against the roof of the flower. The insect then contacts the anthers and becomes covered with pollen as it searches for nectar. The lower lip spots act as nectar guides directing pollinators into the flower.

PARENTUCELLIA
Parentucellia viscosa
Figwort Family (Scrophulariaceae)

Description: Perennial, stems up to 20" tall. The stem hairs are stickier higher up on the stems. The leaves are egg or lance shaped, ½–2" long, and toothed along the margin. Yellow tubular flowers are ½–1" long and borne in an elongated cluster. The lower lip is 3-lobed, while the upper lip curves to form a hood. Fruit is a capsule.

Bloom Season: Mid spring to late summer

Habitat/Range: Introduced from Europe, grows in moist sites at low elevation mostly west of the Cascades.

Comments: *Parentucellia* honors Tomaso Parentucelli (1397–1455), who became Pope Nicholas V and established the Vatican Library and botanical garden. *Viscosa* ("sticky") refers to the hairs on the stems. Bees and very small insects (ants or beetles) probe the flowers for nectar and help to pollinate the flowers.

BRACTED LOUSEWORT
Pedicularis bracteosa
Figwort Family (Scrophulariaceae)

Description: Perennial, often 2–3' tall. The divided, fernlike leaves are 1–5" long and have saw-toothed edges. Flowers arise in a dense, elongated cluster at the end of the flowering stalk. Individual flowers are yellowish to brownish red or purple and have an upper lip that forms a hood and a leaflike bract at their base. The hood may or may not have a short beak. Fruit is a curved capsule.

Bloom Season: Summer

Habitat/Range: Thickets, meadows, forest edges, or open forests from mid to alpine elevations throughout western North America.

Comments: *Pedicularis* is from the Latin *pedicularis* ("relating to lice") after the old belief that grazing livestock became plagued with lice after foraging in fields with a European species of *Pedicularis*. *Bracteosa* ("with well-developed bracts") refers to the flower's leaflike bracts. Also called Wood Betony or Fernleaf.

YELLOW PRAIRIE VIOLET
Viola bakeri
Violet Family (Violaceae)

Description: Perennial. The long-stemmed leaf blades are lance to heart shaped, toothed along the margin and smooth or hairy. The leaves may be 1–5" long. The yellow flowers have 5 lobes; the lower 3 have purple veins, and the upper ones have brownish or purplish backs. Fruit is a capsule.

Bloom Season: Spring

Habitat/Range: Dry meadows, grasslands, prairies, and sagebrush flats from low to mid elevations on the east side of the Cascades from British Columbia to California and east to the Rocky Mountains.

Comments: *Viola* is the Latin name for various sweet-scented flowers, including violets. Goosefoot Violet *(V. purpurea)* is similar with coarsely veined leaves and the upper petals with purplish backs. Another east-side species is Sagebrush Violet *(V. trinervata),* which has compound leaves and purple and yellow, violet-shaped flowers.

GREEN AND BROWN FLOWERS

This section includes flowers that are predominantly brown or green. Some flowers included here also tend toward yellow, lavender, or pale purple. Check those sections if you don't find what you're looking for here.

POISON OAK
Toxicodendron diversiloba
Cashew Family (Anacardiaceae)

Description: Perennial, low-growing shrub or vine with woody stems 6–60" long (more if a vine). The glossy, compound leaves have 3 somewhat rounded leaflets with variable margins and pointed tips. Tiny greenish flowers are borne in open clusters, and may be comprised of male or female flowers, or both. Fruit is a white to yellowish berry.

Bloom Season: Mid spring to early summer

Habitat/Range: Widespread in woodlands and thickets along the west side of the Cascades from Washington to Mexico.

Comments: *Toxicodendron* ("toxic tree") refers to the nonvolatile oil called urushoil found on the leaves and stems that can cause skin irritation. *Diversiloba* ("diverse lobes") is for the variable lobes on the leaves. Poison Ivy *(T. rydbergii)* also has leaves in clusters of 3 that can cause severe skin reactions. Smoke inhalation of either species can drastically affect breathing, due to internal swelling.

WILD GINGER
Asarum caudatum
Birthwort Family (Aristolochiaceae)

Description: Perennial, creeping ground cover. Heart-shaped leaves borne on slender, hairy stalks (velvety to the touch) are 2–5" long. The leaves often cover the flowers and trailing stems. The cup-shaped flower, borne at ground level, has 3 brownish red (sometimes greenish yellow) sepals that are broadly lance-shaped and taper to long points. The sepals are 1–3" long and are fused together at the base. The fruit is an egg-shaped capsule.

Bloom Season: Early to midsummer

Habitat/Range: Moist, shady woods from British Columbia to central California and east to western Montana.

Comments: *Asarum* is from the Greek name for the plant and *caudatum* ("with a tail") refers to the slender tips of the sepals. Though the roots are edible, this plant is not related to the commercially harvested ginger species. Native Indians used the leaves and roots for various ailments, including putting the plant into the bedding of infants to quiet them. Ants or flies pollinate the ground-level flowers. Fungus Gnats lay their eggs in the flowers.

PALLID MILKWEED
Asclepias cryptoceras
Milkweed Family (Asclepiadaceae)

Description: Perennial, stems trail along the ground 4–12". The broad leaves are opposite, smooth and oval. The flowers are borne in loose clusters; the greenish white petals bend backwards exposing a pale rose center. The 5 pouch-shaped hoods protect the stamens. Fruit are 2–3" long, slender seedpods.

Bloom Season: Late spring

Habitat/Range: Dry, gravelly, or sandy sites in southern Washington south to California and east to western Idaho.

Comments: *Asclepias* refers to Asklepios, a mortal physician who was an authority on plants and their healing properties. According to Greek mythology, Asklepios was killed by a thunderbolt from Zeus after he boasted about reviving the dead. *Cryptoceras* is from *krypto* ("hide") and *keras* ("horn") in reference to the flower. The legs of small pollinators become stuck in the hood slits and they cannot break free. Larger pollinators like butterflies or moths can withdraw their legs, which have sacs of pollen wrapped around them.

BEACH SILVERWEED
Ambrosia chamissonis
Sunflower Family (Asteraceae)

Description: Perennial, mat-forming with stems 1–4' long. The spatula-shaped leaves are either deeply dissected or entire with toothed margins. The leaves may be up to 3" long and are covered with dense, white hairs. The male flowering stalk resembles a tassel and bears numerous tiny pollen producing flowers, while the female flowers are usually borne in the leaf axils or found at the base of the tassel. The fruit is a spine-covered seed.

Bloom Season: Summer

Habitat/Range: Beaches and sand dunes along the coast from British Columbia to southern California.

Comments: *Ambrosia* was the food of the gods, making all who ate it immortal. *Chamissonis* is for Adelbert von Chamisso (1781–1838), a French-born German botanist who collected plants in California in 1816. Shifting sands may cover the lower stems.

FALSE AZALEA
Menziesia ferruginea
Heath Family (Ericaceae)

Description: Shrub, up to 6' tall. Young stems have rust-colored sticky hairs that have a foul odor when crushed. The elliptical to ovate leaves are light green, are 1–2" long, have a pointed white leaf tip, and are crowded toward the branch end. The greenish salmon, pink, or yellow urn-shaped flowers hang downwards off short stems and are ¼" long. Fruit is a capsule.

Bloom Season: Late spring and summer

Habitat/Range: Shady, moist sites in coniferous forests and forest edges at low to mid elevations from British Columbia to California and east to Wyoming.

Comments: *Menziesia* honors Archibald Menzies (1754–1842), a Scottish physician and naturalist who accompanied Captain George Vancouver on his 1790–1795 Pacific exploration. *Ferruginea* ("rusty") refers to the color of the hairs on the leaves and stems. Leaves turn yellow or red in the fall.

ONE-SIDED PYROLA
Orthilia secunda
Heath Family (Ericaceae)

Description: Perennial, 2–10" tall. Evergreen basal leaves are ovalish, toothed along the margin and 1–2½" long. The pale green flowers are borne on one side of a leafless flowering stalk. The bell-shaped flowers are about ¼" long with a style that projects straight beyond the flower. Fruit is a rounded capsule.

Bloom Season: Mid to late summer

Habitat/Range: Dry sites in coniferous woods from low to subalpine elevations throughout the region.

Comments: *Orthilia* ("straight spiral") and *secunda* ("side-flowering") refer to the one-sided arrangement of the flowers. The crushed leaves were used as a poultice.

WILD LICORICE
Glycyrrhiza lepidota
Pea Family (Fabaceae)

Description: Perennial, up to 3' tall. The compound leaves have 11–19 elliptical leaflets. Tiny greenish white pea-shaped flowers are borne in dense clusters. Fruit is a seedpod covered with hooked prickles.

Bloom Season: Mid spring to midsummer

Habitat/Range: Sandy areas along streams or disturbed sites at low elevations from British Columbia to California and east to parts of Idaho and Montana.

Comments: *Glycyrrhiza* is from the Greek *glykos* ("sweet") and *rhiza* ("root"), which refers to the taste of the root. *Lepidota* ("scaly") refers to the brown scales on the leaves. Native tribes harvested the roots and ate them raw or roasted. Wild Licorice is still used to treat colds and sore throats.

CHECKER LILY
Fritillaria affinis
Lily Family (Liliaceae)

Description: Perennial from a small fleshy-scaled bulb covered with rice-sized bulblets. The unbranched stems attain 4–40" tall. Lance-shaped linear leaves are borne in whorls at base, pairs along the upper stem. The bowl-shaped mottled flowers that are 1½" wide have purple, yellow, or green mottling on the 6 tepals. Flowers hang downwards and the tepals flare open. Fruit is a many-seeded capsule.

Bloom Season: Late spring to early summer

Habitat/Range: Grassy areas and woodland meadows from low to mid elevations from British Columbia to California and east to northern Idaho.

Comments: *Fritillary* ("dice box") refers to the capsules and *affinis* ("similar to") refers to the similarity of the flowers to other *Fritillaria* species. Flowers have a somewhat foul aroma. Also called Mission Bells or Rice-Root Lily, after the small bulblets attached to the roots.

SMALL GROUND-CONE
Boschniakia hookeri
Broomrape Family (Orobanchaceae)

Description: Parasitic plant, 4–6" tall. Resembles an upright yellow to dark maroon pinecone. Succulent stems covered with scalelike leaves. The 2-lipped flowers arise between bracts at the terminal end of the stem. The flowers are slender and yellow to purple and have unequal lips. Fruit is a many-seeded capsule.

Bloom Season: Late spring and early summer

Habitat/Range: Forest duff and coastal woodlands from Alaska to northern California.

Comments: *Boschniakia* is for Alexander Karlovick Boschniak (1786–1831), a Russian botanist. *Hookeri* is for either one or both of the British botanists: Sir William J. Hooker and his son, Sir Joseph Dalton Hooker (1817–1911). The fleshy roots contact and draw nutrients from their host plants, which include Salal *(Gaultheria shallon)* and Kinnickinick *(Arctostaphylos uva-ursi)*.

CLUSTERED BROOMRAPE
Orobanche fasiculata
Broomrape Family (Orobanchaceae)

Description: Parasitic, clustered stems up to 8" tall. The leaves are scalelike along the flowering stem. The tubular flowers are purplish, often with a yellow tinge, and ½–¾" long. The 2-lipped flower has 2 upper lobes and 3 lower lobes. Fruit is a capsule.

Bloom Season: Summer

Habitat/Range: Sagebrush plains, open forests from low to mid elevations throughout the drier portions of the region.

Comments: *Orobanche* is from *orobos* ("clinging plant"), and *ancho* ("to strangle") refers to the parasitic nature of this plant. *Fasiculata* ("clustered") refers to the stems. The common name arises from a European species that is parasitic on Scotch Broom, but Clustered Broomrape often parasitizes sagebrushes *(Artemesia* spp.).

GIANT HELLEBORINE
Epipactis gigantea
Orchid Family (Orchidaceae)

Description: Perennial from spreading underground roots. Upright stems 1–2' but may reach 5'. Stems bear numerous oval- to lance-shaped leaves that are 2–8" long. The greenish to purplish flowers have 3½"-long greenish sepals and 3 petals with purple or dull red lines. The upper petals are smaller and greenish purple, and the lower petal is pouchlike and pinched in the middle to form a 3-lobed tip with a curled margin. Fruit is a capsule.

Bloom Season: Mid spring to midsummer

Habitat/Range: Springs, seeps, streambanks, and moist sites from desert regions to woodlands across southern British Columbia to Baja California and east to the Rocky Mountains.

Comments: *Epipactis* is from the ancient Greek name *epipaktis* ("helleborine"), and *gigantea* ("large") refers to the stature of the plant. Wasps are the primary pollinators of these orchids, attracted in great numbers by scent. The flowers also self-pollinate.

HEART-LEAVED TWAYBLADE
Listera cordata
Orchid Family (Orchidaceae)

Description: Perennial; grows 2–10" tall but may be overlooked. The 2 stem leaves are heart shaped, 1–2½" long and clasp the stem at the same midlength point. The yellowish green or purplish brown flowers are ⅛–½" long and 2 lipped. The slightly inflated flowers have a lower lip that is deeply divided for half its length. Fruit is a capsule.

Bloom Season: Mid spring to early summer

Habitat/Range: Moist, mossy coniferous forests at mid elevations throughout the region and into Eurasia.

Comments: *Listera* honors the English naturalist Martin Lister (1638–1712), and *cordata* ("heart-shaped") refers to the shape of the leaves. Various species of flies, wasps, and Fungus Gnats are attracted to the foul-smelling flowers. When they land upon the center column of the flower, a sticky mass of pollen explodes from the stamens and "glues" itself to their legs. The pollen either falls or is scraped off at another flower. Twayblade ("two-blades") refers to the 2 leaves.

BROWN'S PEONY
Paeonia brownii
Peony Family (Paeoniaceae)

Description: Perennial, 8–24" tall. Fleshy leaves are compound once or twice and the leaflets are deeply lobed. The heavy blossoms, 3–4" wide, weigh the stems down often to the ground. Five to 6 oval, green or reddish sepals surround 5–10 white to maroon petals that are edged with yellow. The numerous stamens surround the styles that elongate in fruit. Fruit is a 2–3" seedpod.

Bloom Season: Mid to late spring

Habitat/Range: Sagebrush plains, open pine woodlands, and meadow edges at mid elevations from central Washington to Idaho and south to California.

Comments: *Paeonia* is for Paeon, the Greek physician to the gods. *Brownii* honors Robert Brown (1773–1858). These peonies produce abundant pollen but little nectar, but still attract bees, wasps, and ants as pollinators.

SEASIDE PLANTAIN
Plantago maritima
Plantain Family (Plantaginaceae)

Description: Perennial, often low-growing but may reach 1' tall. Basal cluster of linear leaves are tough, 2–3" in length, and smooth (toothed in one variety) along the margin. The upright flowering stalk, 1–5" long, bears numerous tiny 4-petaled flowers with hairy corollas. Fruit is a seed.

Bloom Season: Summer

Habitat/Range: Rock outcrops, bluffs, or beach edges along the coast from Alaska to southern California.

Comments: *Plantago* is the Latin name for this genus, and *maritima* ("maritime") refers to the coastal distribution. The young leaves are edible either raw or steamed. Several other species of *Plantago* occur along the coast. The stamens protrude beyond the flowers and, like many plantains, may be both wind and insect pollinated.

DAVIS' KNOTWEED
Polygonum davisiae
Polygonum Family (Polygonaceae)

Description: Perennial with nonwoody, reddish stems that often spread along the ground. The fleshy, oval- to egg-shaped leaves, 1–3" long, are borne on short stems and taper to a point. Small greenish white to pink flowers are borne in leaf axils in small clusters.

Bloom Season: Summer

Habitat/Range: Open, rocky slopes at subalpine elevations from Washington to central California and east to central Idaho.

Comments: *Polygonum* is from the Greek *poly* ("many") and *gonu* ("knee") in reference to the swollen kneelike nodes of some species. *Davisiae* honors Nancy Jane Davis (1833–1921). Also called Newberry's Fleeceflower after John Strong Newberry (1822–1892).

SEASIDE DOCK
Rumex maritimus
Buckwheat Family (Polygonaceae)

Description: Annual, the 8–20" long stems sprawl across the ground. The leaf blades are lance shaped to broadly linear, 2–7" long, and wavy along the margins. The tiny greenish brown flowers are borne in clusters in leaf axils; the flowers are less than ⅛" long. Fruit is a single-seeded nut with sandlike swellings on the surface.

Bloom Season: Summer and early autumn

Habitat/Range: Coastal beaches and wet saline areas throughout the region and to the Northeast. Also found in South America and Eurasia.

Comments: *Rumex* is the Latin name for sorrel or dock. *Maritimus* ("maritime") refers to the coastal or saline environments where these plants grow. Also called Golden Dock after the color of the stems at maturity.

WESTERN MEADOW RUE
Thalictrum occidentalis
Buttercup Family (Ranunculaceae)

Description: Perennial, stems 1–3' tall. The compound leaves divide several times, and the 1" wide leaflets are smooth with 3 scalloped lobes. Male and female flowers borne on separate plants. Male flowers have numerous yellow stamens and brown to purple filaments that hang downwards. Female flowers are tiny, green to purplish, and arranged in clusters. Fruit is a hairless seed.

Bloom Season: Mid spring to midsummer

Habitat/Range: Moist woods and meadows at low to mid elevations from British Columbia to California and east to the Rocky Mountains.

Comments: *Thalictrum* is the Greek name for this plant, and *occidentalis* ("western") refers to the plant's distribution. Often confused for a grass.

CALIFORNIA PITCHER PLANT
Darlingtonia californica
Pitcher Plant Family (Sarraceniaceae)

Description: Perennial, insectivorous plants. Large leaves, 5–20" long, are hood shaped and greenish yellow with purple spots on the hood. At the base of the hood is an opening that has 2 moustachelike bracts. A single, 2" long flower is borne on a leafless stalk that is 1–3' tall. The flowers have cream-colored sepals and purplish petals, and the flowers hang downwards. Fruit is a turban-shaped capsule.

Bloom Season: Mid spring through summer

Habitat/Range: Often in nitrogen-poor locations such as bogs and springs and along small streams from sea level to mid elevations in southwest Oregon to northern California. Best viewed at the Darlingtonia Botanical Wayside just north of Florence, Oregon.

Comments: *Darlingtonia* is for Dr. William Darlington (1782–1863), a Philadelphia botanist. *Californica* ("of California") refers to its type location. Flies, wasps, bees, ants, and beetles are attracted to the nectar source within the opening. As the insects attempt to leave, the opaque spots on the hood confuse them. The insects tire, since the inner surface is smooth and has downward pointing hairs to prevent landing. The insects fall into the digestive fluid at the leaf base and are digested by enzymes. Small tree frogs may also fall prey to these leaves. Also called Cobra Plant. Round-Leaved Sundew *(Drosera rotundifolia)* is another insectivorous plant but with round leaves that close together to trap and consume prey.

LEAFY MITREWORT
Mitella caulescens
Saxifrage Family (Saxifragaceae)

Description: Perennials that grow up to 25" tall. The basal leaves are broad and 5-lobed—the lobes are finely toothed along the margins. Upper stem leaves are smaller. Greenish flowers have 5 stamens, are ⅛–¼" long, saucer shaped, and have petals with fringelike feathery tips. Fruit is a capsule.

Bloom Season: Spring and early summer

Habitat/Range: Moist woods and meadows or along streambanks at mid elevations from British Columbia to northern California and east to Montana.

Comments: *Mitella* is from the Greek *mitra* ("a cap") and refers to the form of the developing fruit. *Caulescens* ("having a stem") may refer to the leaves along the flowering stalk. The flowers of Leafy Mitrewort mature from the top to the bottom. Naked Mitrewort *(M. nuda)* has 10 stamens, and Feathery Mitrewort *(M. breweri)* has only round, basal leaves that are heart shaped at the base.

YOUTH-ON-AGE
Tolmiea menziesii
Saxifrage Family (Saxifragaceae)

Description: Perennial; grows 1– 2½' tall. The basal leaves arise on long stalks covered with soft hairs. The lobes on the broad leaves arise from a common point (palmately) and are hairy. A long floral stalk bears numerous greenish purple to brownish flowers that are ⅓–½" long and have a narrow corolla. The thin petals curl at the tips. The fruit is a capsule.

Bloom Season: Mid spring to midsummer

Habitat/Range: Plants grow in moist, shady forests or open areas from low to mid elevations from Alaska to California west of the Cascades.

Comments: *Tolmiea* is for William Frazier Tolmie (1830–1886), a Scottish doctor who worked for the Hudson Bay Company in the Northwest and also collected plants in the region. *Menziesii* is for Archibald Menzies (1754–1842), the English surgeon-naturalist who sailed with Captain George Vancouver in 1792 to explore the Northwest coast. The common name refers to the vegetative reproductive ability of these plants. Young plants arise from buds located at the base of the "adult" leaf.

137

LANCE-LEAF FIGWORT
Scrophularia lanceolata
Figwort Family (Scrophulariaceae)

Description: Perennial with 4-angled stems, 1–3' tall. The long leaves are toothed along the margin, long stemmed with triangular, egg-shaped blades. The 2-lipped flowers are greenish yellow with maroon, about ½" long and slightly inflated. The upper 2-lobed lip projects over the lower 3-lobed lip. Fruit is a capsule.

Bloom Season: Early to midsummer

Habitat/Range: Moist sites along streams and clearings at low elevations from British Columbia to California.

Comments: *Scrophularia* is from the Latin *scrofule* ("scrophula") after the plant's medicinal usage to treat swollen glands. *Lanceolata* ("lance-shaped") refers to the leaves. California Figwort (S. californica) has brownish to maroon-colored flowers.

STINGING NETTLE
Urtica dioica
Nettle Family (Urticaceae)

Description: Perennial from creeping roots with stems 3–9' tall. Stems and leaves are covered with stinging hairs. Leaves are opposite, broadly lance to egg shaped and with saw-toothed margins. Clusters of tiny, nondescript greenish flowers borne in the upper leaf axils. The flowers may be all male, all female, or have both male and female appendages. Fruit is a flat, oval seed.

Bloom Season: Summer

Habitat/Range: Moist sites along streams, rivers, thickets, and woodlands from sea level to subalpine elevations throughout the region.

Comments: *Uro* ("to burn") is the Latin name for nettle. *Dioica* ("dioecious") refers to the male and female flowers borne on separate plants. The stem fibers were plaited into cordage. The cooked stems and leaves were, and still are, eaten as "wild spinach." The hollow hairs contain formic acid, which, when crushed or broken, irritates the skin. Pollen is wind dispersed as the plants bloom in summer.

BLUE AND PURPLE FLOWERS

This section includes flowers that range
in color from pale blue to deep indigo and
violet. Since these colors grade into pink
and lavender, and since some plants
produce flowers that range across all of
these colors, you should check among the
pink flowers in the red and violet section if
you don't find the flower you are looking for
here.

ALPINE ASTER
Oreostemma alpigenum
Sunflower Family (Asteraceae)

Description: Perennial, 4–10" tall. Basal leaves linear and 2–7" long. The stem leaves are smaller. The 1–3 stems bear a single floral head, about 1½" wide. Heads made of bluish purple ray and yellow disk flowers. The petals are often twisted or drooping. Fruit is a seed with hairs.

Bloom Season: Summer

Habitat/Range: Moist meadows or open forests at subalpine to alpine elevations from Washington to California and east to the northern Rocky Mountains.

Comments: *Oreostemma* is from *oros* ("mountain") and *stemma* ("a garland"), and *alpigenum* ("alpine") refers to the plant's distribution. Blooms in profusion.

CUSHION FLEABANE
Erigeron poliospermus
Sunflower Family (Asteraceae)

Description: Perennial, cushionlike, 2–6" tall. Narrow or spatula-shaped leaves are 1–1½" long and covered with dense hairs. Flowering stalks also bear numerous hairs and usually end with a single floral cluster, although the stalks may branch. Flower heads are 1" wide and have 25–30 pink or lavender ray flowers (sometimes white) surrounding a cluster of yellow disk flowers. Fruit is a seed with numerous white hairs.

Bloom Season: Spring

Habitat/Range: Dry rocky sites or slopes in sagebrush habitats from southern British Columbia to central Oregon and east to western Idaho.

Comments: *Erigeron* is from the Greek words *eri* ("early") and *geron* ("an old man"), which refers to the white seed heads. *Poliospermus* ("gray seed") refers to the long hairs on the seed.

CASCADE ASTER
Eucephalus ledophyllus
Sunflower Family (Asteraceae)

Description: Perennial, 10–30". Unbranched stems bear numerous 1–4" long egg- to broadly lance-shaped leaves with the larger leaves along the middle portion of the stem. Each stem bears several daisylike flower heads that have 6–21 lavender to bluish purple ray flowers surrounding a center of yellowish disk flowers. Fruit is a seed with tawny bristles.

Bloom Season: Midsummer to fall

Habitat/Range: Dry or moist meadows, forest openings, or edges at mid to subalpine elevations on the east side of the Cascades from British Columbia to California.

Comments: *Eucephalus* comes from Greek for "good head." *Ledophyllus* ("rockrose leaf") refers to the lower leaves resembling those of Labrador Tea. Leafy Aster *(Symphyotrichum cusickii)* has large, long-stemmed, spoon-shaped leaves and occurs on either side of the Cascades.

PACIFIC HOUND'S TONGUE
Cynoglossum grande
Borage Family (Boraginaceae)

Description: Perennial with stout stems; may be 1–3' tall. Large lance-shaped to oval leaf blades are 3–8" long and are borne on long stems. The leaves have a rough texture. The dark blue flowers arise on a stout flowering stalk and are about ½" wide. Five petals fuse together to form a short tube that flares open and surrounds a white center collar. Fruit is a nutlet with hooked prickles at the tip.

Bloom Season: Mid to late spring

Habitat/Range: Woods and forest edges in low to mid elevation sites from southern British Columbia to central California on the west side of the Cascades, but in the Columbia River Gorge also.

Comments: *Cynoglossum* is from the Greek words *kyon* ("dog") and *glossum* ("tongue") in reference to the large leaves. *Grande* ("large") refers to the leaves of this striking plant.

LEAFY BLUEBELL
Mertensia oblongifolia
Borage Family (Boraginaceae)

Description: Perennial, with clustered stems up to 16" tall. Basal leaves, 2–3" long, have long stems and an elliptical blade. Bluish flowers are borne in a tight cluster and have a tube that ends in 5 shallow lobes. Fruits are nutlets.

Bloom Season: Late spring to early summer

Habitat/Range: Open areas or forest edges from low to subalpine elevations throughout the region, east of the Cascades.

Comments: *Mertensia* honors Franz Karl Mertens (1764–1831), a botany professor in Bremen, Germany. *Oblongifolia* ("oblong leaves") refers to the shape of the leaves.

TALL BLUEBELLS
Mertensia paniculata
Borage Family (Boraginaceae)

Description: Perennial, with several stout stems 10–60" tall. The basal leaves are egg to heart shaped and long stalked, while the stem leaves are lance to egg shaped and may be stalkless. Leaves are hairy above and sometimes hairy below. Bell-shaped flowers are borne in clusters; each flower is ½–1" long and tube shaped at the base. Flowers are pinkish when first opening and change color to blue with maturity. Fruits are 4 nutlets joined together.

Bloom Season: Early summer

Habitat/Range: Wetter sites in meadows, open forests, and along streambanks from low to high elevations mainly east of the Cascades from British Columbia to Oregon and east to Idaho.

Comments: *Mertensia* honors Franz Karl Mertens (1764–1831), a botany professor in Bremen, Germany. His son Karl Heinrich Mertens (1796–1830), who collected plants on an Alaskan expedition in 1827, named the genus for his father. *Paniculata* ("in a panicle") refers to the floral arrangement.

COMMON BLUEBELL
Campanula rotundifolia
Harebell Family (Campanulaceae)

Description: Perennial, often growing in clumps 6–18" tall. Rounded to heart-shaped basal leaves wither before the flowers open and the few stem leaves are narrow. Blue, bell-shaped flowers are ¾" long and have 5 petals. Fruit is a capsule.

Bloom Season: Summer

Habitat/Range: Open areas, meadows, and forest edges from low to subalpine elevations throughout the mountains of North America.

Comments: *Campanula* is from the Latin *campana* ("bell"), which refers to the flower shape, *Rotundifolia* ("round leaved") refers to the shape of the basal leaves. Insects may overnight in the closed flowers, protected from the elements. As the wind rattles the capsules, the seeds escape through small slits. Also called Scotch Bluebell or Lady's Thimble, this plant is widely used in cultivated rock gardens.

SCOULER'S BLUEBELL
Campanula scouleri
Harebell Family (Campanulaceae)

Description: Perennial, with weak stems 4–15" tall. Basal leaves rounded, toothed along the margin and borne on long stems. Upper leaves more narrow and lance shaped than the basal ones. The bell-shaped, pale blue to violet-colored flowers are ¼–½" long. The petals form a short tube that ends with the petals curving up and backwards. A single style extends beyond the petals and ends with a thickened stigma. The fruit is a capsule.

Bloom Season: Late spring to midsummer

Habitat/Range: Moist, shady forests or open slopes from Alaska to northern California, mostly west of the Cascades.

Comments: *Campanula* is from the Latin *campana* ("a bell") and refers to the flower shape of this genus. *Scouleri* is for John Scouler (1804–1871), a Scotsman who joined the British Navy as a surgeon and who botanized with David Douglas in the Northwest. The plants are either pollinated by insects or may be self-pollinated. Piper's Bellflower *(C. piperi)* is a small bellflower that grows on talus slopes in the Olympic Mountains.

BEACH PEA
Lathyrus japonicus
Pea Family (Fabaceae)

Description: Perennial, with stems reaching 4' long. Stems either on the ground or climbing. The compound leaves have 6–12 leaflets that are smooth. Two large triangular, leaflike stipules arise at the base of the leaves, and the leaves end in a tendril. The 1" long purplish pea-shaped flowers are borne in loose clusters. The upper petal is enlarged. Fruit is a pod.

Bloom Season: Summer

Habitat/Range: Coastal beaches and fore-dunes from Alaska to northern California, as well as coastal Japan.

Comments: *Lathyrus* is from the Greek name for peas—*lathyros*. *Japonicus* ("of Japan") refers to the plant's distribution. The seedpod is edible. Silky Beach Pea *(L. littoralis)* also grows along the coast and has edible roots and smaller leaves with dense hairs. Beach Pea is bee pollinated.

PRAIRIE LUPINE
Lupinus aridus
Pea Family (Fabaceae)

Description: Perennial, up to 14" tall. The basal, compound leaves have long stems and 5–7 inversely lance-shaped leaflets that have silvery hairs below. The blue to light purple flowers are borne in dense elongated clusters. The pea-shaped flowers are small and have a white mark on the upper petal. Fruit is a seedpod.

Bloom Season: Summer

Habitat/Range: Dry sites in open areas, sagebrush flats or pine forests from low to alpine elevations throughout the region east of the Cascades.

Comments: *Lupinus* is from *lupus* ("wolf") due to the misconception that lupines "wolf" nourishment from the soil. *Aridus* ("arid") refers to the dry areas these plants inhabit. Dwarf Lupine *(L. pusillus)* is another low-growing, dry-region lupine but it is an annual. Prairie Lupine may also be called Alpine Lupine.

BROADLEAF LUPINE
Lupinus latifolius
Pea Family (Fabaceae)

Description: Perennial, often in clumps, 1–3' tall, and in profusion. Leaves are palmately compound with 7–9 broadly egg-shaped or elliptical leaflets that are usually hairy. Flowers borne in a dense cluster on an elongated stalk. The blue to purplish flowers arise on short stalks and have a smooth, bent-backwards upper petal and broad side petals. Fruit are hairy pods.

Bloom Season: Late spring and early summer

Habitat/Range: Widespread in moist or damp meadows, roadsides, and forest edges or openings from low to subalpine elevations east of the Cascades.

Comments: *Lupinus* is from *lupus* ("wolf") due to the misconception that lupines "wolf" nourishment from the soil. *Latifolius* ("broad leaf") describes the leaf size. Bees are the primary pollinators of many lupines, as they can force their way into the flowers. Many-Leaved Lupine *(L. polyphyllus)* is another tall lupine with large leaves up to 8" wide.

SPURRED LUPINE
Lupinus laxiflorus
Pea Family (Fabaceae)

Description: Perennial, 20" tall. Leaves are divided into narrow segments The bluish violet (sometimes white to reddish) flowers are borne on an elongated stalk. The ½"-long flowers have a blunt spur on the calyx and side petals that are hairy at the tip. Fruit is a pod.

Bloom Season: Mid spring to early summer

Habitat/Range: Dry, sagebrush flats, grasslands, or pine forests at low to mid elevations on the east side of the Cascades from Washington to California and east into Idaho and Utah.

Comments: *Lupinus* is from *lupus* ("wolf") due to the misconception that lupines "wolf" nourishment from the soil. *Laxiflorus* ("loose-flowered") refers to the open cluster of flowers.

SHORE LUPINE
Lupinus littoralis
Pea Family (Fabaceae)

Description: Perennial with mostly trailing stems that may reach 2' long. Compound leaves bear 5 to 8 lance-shaped leaflets that are 1" long. Pea-shaped flowers borne in dense clusters; the lower petals are bluish while the upper petal is whiter with small black dots at the base.

Bloom Season: Mid spring to late summer

Habitat/Range: Sandy beaches and coastal bluffs from British Columbia to northern California.

Comments: *Lupinus* is from *lupus* ("wolf") due to the misconception that lupines "wolf" nourishment from the soil. *Littoralis* ("shore") refers to the plant's coastal distribution. Coastal tribes ate the fleshy roots. Bumblebees pollinate these flowers.

WHITESTEM FRASERA

Frasera albicaulis
Gentian Family (Gentinaceae)

Description: Perennial, 10–30" tall. Basal leaves long, linear, up to 6", with white margins. Upper leaves smaller and opposite. Flower clusters borne at the end of an elongated stalk. Blue (rarely white) flowers, ½" wide, with 4 lance-shaped, mottled petals. The petals have a hair-lined gland at their base. Fruit is a small capsule.

Bloom Season: Late spring to midsummer

Habitat/Range: Meadows and open woods of the lower mountains from British Columbia to Montana and south to Northwest California on the east side of the Cascades.

Comments: *Frasera* honors John Fraser (1750–1811), a Scottish botanist and explorer who collected plants in America and Cuba in the 18th century. *Albicaulis* ("white-stemmed") refers to the edges of the leaves. Several varieties exist.

NARROW-LEAF PHACELIA
Phacelia linearis
Waterleaf Family (Hydrophyllaceae)

Description: Annual. Plants grow 5–20" tall. Basal leaves are narrow and the larger, upper leaves may have split into 1–4 narrow segments. Showy, light blue flowers are ½–1" wide and have 5 petals. The flower buds are arranged in a coiled pattern. Fruit is a rough-textured seed.

Bloom Season: Late spring and early summer

Habitat/Range: Open areas in dry low to mid elevation sites on the east side of the Cascades.

Comments: *Phacelia* ("fascicle") refers to the tightly clustered flowers. *Linearis* ("linear") describes the leaf shape. The dishlike flowers attract bees, flies, and beetles as pollinators.

WESTERN BLUE FLAG
Iris missouriensis
Iris Family (Iridaceae)

Description: Perennial, with grasslike leaves. Atop the 1–2' stems are a pair (sometimes 4) of pale blue flowers about 3" wide. The showy flowers have 3 wide sepals lined with purplish streaks and a yellow base, 3 upright petals and 3 petal-like styles. Fruit is a large capsule.

Bloom Season: Late spring to midsummer

Habitat/Range: Moist, marshy areas or along streams from low to mid elevations from Alaska to Baja California and east to Minnesota.

Comments: *Iris* honors the Greek goddess Iris, whose message-bearing appearance was heralded by a rainbow. *Missouriensis* ("of the Missouri River") is from Meriwether Lewis who collected this plant along the Missouri. Native Americans used the pulverized roots of the Western Blue Flag to treat toothaches, and the stems and leaves were used in making weavings or cordage strong enough to snare an elk. Also called Missouri Iris. Bumblebees land on the wide sepal and push their way under the petal-like segment to suck nectar, pollinating the flower in the process.

OREGON FLAG
Iris tenax
Iris Family (Iridaceae)

Description: Perennial to 20" tall. The basal grasslike leaves are up to 20" long but narrow. Stem leaves are smaller. The showy flowers range from blue to purple and may be white, pink, yellow, or lavender. The sepals have yellow and white centers and dark purple veins; the petals are narrower and solid in color. Fruit is an angled capsule that splits open into 3 chambers.

Bloom Season: Spring to early summer

Habitat/Range: Grassy meadows, open fields, roadsides, and open forests at low to mid elevations from Washington to California on the west side of the Cascades.

Comments: *Iris* honors the Greek goddess Iris, whose message-bearing appearance was heralded by a rainbow. *Tenax* ("tough") refers to the durability of the leaves. The Scottish botanist David Douglas collected and named this plant after observing native tribes in California making fishing nets and snares from the leaves to trap fish, deer, and bear.

BLUE-EYED GRASS
Sisyrinchium idahoense
Iris Family (Iridaceae)

Description: Perennial, flattened stems are up to 14" tall. The mostly basal leaves are long and linear—grasslike. The 1"-wide flowers arise individually or in small clusters and are blue to bluish purple with a yellow center. The 6 tepals are pointed at the tip. Fruit is a rounded or egg-shaped capsule.

Bloom Season: Late spring to midsummer

Habitat/Range: Grows in moist meadows and seasonally (spring) wet areas in juniper and Ponderosa Pine forests at low to mid elevations from Alaska south to Baja California, across Canada to east side of the Rocky Mountains.

Comments: *Sisyrinchium* is the ancient Greek name for a different plant. *Idahoense* ("of Idaho") refers to the type locality. The common name refers to the grasslike leaves.

FIELD MINT
Mentha arvensis
Mint Family (Laminaceae)

Description: Perennial, with square stems, 1–3' tall. The opposite leaves are broadly lance-shaped, 1–3" long, and toothed along the margin. The leaves extend beyond the flower clusters. The purplish to pink or white flowers are borne in small clusters in the upper leaf axils. The tiny flowers have 4 stamens that protrude above the flowers. Fruit is a tiny nutlet.

Bloom Season: Summer

Habitat/Range: Moist sites in fields, meadows, streams, marshes, and coastal flats from sea level to mid elevations throughout the region and most of North America.

Comments: *Mentha* is named after the Greek nymph Menthe who was transformed into a mint plant by a jealous Persephone. *Arvensis* ("growing near fields") refers to the type of habitat where this plant occurs. The leaves were brewed for a tea to aid digestion or for colds.

SELF-HEAL
Prunella vulgaris
Mint Family (Laminaceae)

Description: Perennial, with square stems 6–36"
tall. The opposite leaves are broadly lance-
shaped to elliptical. The flowers are borne in
dense clusters of purple to blue, 2-lipped flowers.
The lower lip has 3 lobes and fringe on the
middle lobe. The upper lobe forms a flat hood.
Fruit is a nutlet.

Bloom Season: Summer

Habitat/Range: Disturbed sites such as
roadsides, fields, ditches, and other open areas
from low to mid elevations throughout the region.

Comments: The origin of *Prunella* is unclear
because German herbalists in the 15th and 16th
centuries interchanged the names *Prunella* and
Brunella. Vulgaris ("common") refers to the
widespread abundance of this plant. Self-Heal, as
the name implies, was used medicinally to treat
cuts, bruises, rashes, and other skin
inflammations.

NARROW-LEAVED SKULLCAP
Scutellaria angustifolia
Mint Family (Laminaceae)

Description: Perennial with square stems, up to
20". Leaves are opposite and oval to lance shaped
with smooth edges. The 1"-long bluish purple
flowers arise singularly or in pairs from the upper
leaf axils and are tube-shaped. The lower petal is
broad and hairy, while the upper petal forms a
hood or hump. Two smaller side petals border the
outside of the tube. Calyx is 2 lipped and forms a
crest on the upper portion. Fruit is a hard nutlet.

Bloom Season: Late spring to midsummer

Habitat/Range: Dry plains, canyons, and foothills
from low to the mid elevations from southern
British Columbia south to California and Idaho.

Comments: *Scutellaria* is from the Latin word
scutella ("saucer or small dish"), which refers to
the pouch on the upper side of the calyx.
Angustifolia ("narrow-leaved") refers to the shape
of the leaves, which often appear folded
lengthwise. Marsh Skullcap *(S. galericulata)*
grows in wet meadows or marshes and has white
streaks on the blue or pinkish purple flowers.
Lewis and Clark collected this specimen on June
5, 1806, near present-day Kamiah, Idaho.

HARVEST BRODIAEA
Brodiaea coronaria
Lily Family (Liliaceae)

Description: Perennial. Narrow, grasslike leaves are long and often wither before flowering. The 5–16" long stems bear 2–10 bluish purple flowers (white rarely) with the petals curving backwards. The 1"-long flowers have distinctive purple stripes down the center of the petals. Three sterile white stamens resemble small petals.

Bloom Season: Early to midsummer

Habitat/Range: Prairies, grassy meadows, and rocky bluffs at low to mid elevations from Vancouver Island to California and into eastern Oregon and Washington.

Comments: *Brodiaea* honors James Brodie (1744–1824), a Scottish botanist. *Coronaria* ("crowned") refers to the flower arrangement. The common name refers to Native Americans and early settlers who harvested the small, tasty bulbs.

GREEN-BANDED STAR TULIP

Calochortus macrocarpus
Lily Family (Liliaceae)

Description: Perennial, 8–21" tall. The 1–3 grass-like leaves are thin but not flat. One to three flowers are borne on each plant and the flowers are 2" wide. The flowers are lavender, purple, or white, with 3 narrow, pointed sepals that are longer than the 3 broad petals. A green stripe extends down the petals to the sepals. There are reddish purple nectar lines on the lower, inner portion of the petals. Fruit is a capsule.

Bloom Season: Late spring to midsummer

Habitat/Range: Dry meadows, sagebrush flats, or Ponderosa Pine forests from low to high elevations from southern British Columbia to California and east to Montana.

Comments: *Calochortus* ("beautiful grass") refers to the grasslike leaves. *Macrocarpus* ("large-fruited") refers to the large seed capsules. The onionlike bulbs are edible. David Douglas, the Scottish botanist, first recorded the plant in the 1830s. Also called Sagebrush or Large-Flowered Mariposa Lily.

COMMON CAMAS
Camassia quamash
Lily Family (Liliaceae)

Description: Bulb is egg shaped. Grasslike basal leaves are about 1" wide and may grow 2' long. The flowering stalk may bear numerous pale to deep blue (sometimes white) flowers that are roughly 1½" long; 5 of the tepals curve upwards, 1 downwards. Fruit is an egg-shaped capsule that splits open into 3 segments.

Bloom Season: Late spring

Habitat/Range: Low to mid elevations in grassy plains or meadows from British Columbia to California and east to Wyoming and Utah.

Comments: Scientific name is from the Native American names *camas* or *quamash*. Camas bulbs were an important food source for native tribes. The bulbs were dug with digging sticks and roasted in large pits.

BLUE FLAX
Linum lewisii
Flax Family (Linaceae)

Description: Perennial, sometimes with a woody base. Thin, smooth stems grow 1–2' tall and bear linear to lance-shaped leaves that are 1–2" long. The 1"-wide flowers have 5 blue petals that are streaked with purple and 5 styles that protrude beyond the stamens. Fruit is a rounded capsule.

Bloom Season: Mid spring to summer

Habitat/Range: Widespread in western North America in damp or dry meadows or forest openings. Cultivated.

Comments: *Linum* is the Latin name for flax, and *lewisii* is for Captain Meriwether Lewis (1774–1809), co-leader of the Corps of Discovery. Lewis collected and described Blue Flax on his western expedition noting its perennial habit and potential commercial properties. Some western Native tribes used flax fibers to make cordage for nets and snares, while fibers from the cultivated Common Flax *(L. usitatissimum)* have been woven into linen for over 5,000 years.

HOWELL'S TRITELEIA
Triteleia grandiflora
Lily Family (Liliaceae)

Description: Perennial, plants up to 2' tall. Bears 2 grasslike leaves that may reach 1' long. Stems are unbranched, and the flowers are borne in terminal clusters. Tube-shaped flowers have dark blue tubes and lighter blue to white flaring lobes—each flower is about 1" long. Each of the 6 tepals has a dark blue centerline; inner tepals have more wavy edges than outer ones. Fruit is a capsule.

Bloom Season: Mid spring to early summer

Habitat/Range: Grasslands and sagebrush foothills from coast of Southern British Columbia to southwest Oregon on the east side of the Cascades.

Comments: *Triteleia* is from the Greek *tri* ("three") and *teleios* ("perfect") in reference to the floral parts in 3s. *Grandiflora* ("large flowers") are for the sizeable flowers. The common name is for Thomas Howell (1842–1912), who collected plants in Washington and Oregon and wrote *Flora of Northwest America* (1897–1903). Bees, butterflies, small beetles, and perhaps hummingbirds pollinate the long tubular flowers. Bulbs are edible. Also called Bicolored Cluster Lily due to color contrasts on flowers.

NAKED BROOMRAPE
Orobanche uniflora
Cancer-Root Family (Orobanchaceae)

Description: Parasitic plant, 1–4" tall. Leaves are basal, lance shaped and up to ½" long. The long, yellowish flowering stalk has sticky hairs and bears a single flower. The tubular flowers are bluish or purple, 2" long, and have 2 prominent yellow ridges on the lower lip. Fruit is a capsule.

Bloom Season: Early spring to midsummer

Habitat/Range: Moist (at least in spring) meadows, grasslands, open areas, and open woods from low to mid elevations across much of North America.

Comments: *Orobanche* is from *orobos* ("a type of vetch or climbing plant") and *ancho* ("to strangle") referring to the parasitic nature. *Uniflora* ("one flower") indicates the solitary flower, which is borne on a leafless or naked flowering stalk. This species parasitizes species of stonecrop, saxifrage, and some Asteraceae members. A dumbbell-shaped stigma (often yellow) on the upper inside roof of the flower resembles an anther and encourages the insect pollinator to advance into the flower.

BALLHEAD GILIA
Gilia capitata
Phlox Family (Polemoniaceae)

Description: Annual, with thin stems 1–3' tall. Basal and stem leaves are divided into narrow, linear segments. The lower, larger leaves may be 5" long. The ¼–½" wide blue flowers are arranged in rounded clusters. The 5 petals form a short tube then flare outwards. Fruit is a somewhat rounded capsule.

Bloom Season: Summer

Habitat/Range: Open fields, meadows, rocky outcrops, and disturbed areas at low to mid elevations from Washington to California and east to northern Idaho.

Comments: *Gilia* honors Filippo Luigi Gilii (1756–1821), an Italian naturalist and director of the Vatican Observatory who coauthored books about South American plants. *Capitata* ("dense head") refers to the clustered arrangement of the flowers. Also called Many-Flowered or Bluefield Gilia. Butterflies, bees, wasps, and flies are attracted to the abundant flowers.

MENZIES' LARKSPUR
Delphinium menziesii
Buttercup Family (Ranunculaceae)

Description: Perennial, 6–24" tall plants. Basal leaves are deeply divided like the fingers on a hand, and lobed on the edges of the segments. Basal leaves usually are withered prior to flowering. Flowering stalks bear deep blue to purplish flowers comprised of 5 showy petal-like sepals and 4 petals. The upper 2 petals are small and white, while the lower 2 are darker. The upper sepal forms a ½" long spur that projects straight back. Fruit is a pod that splits open at maturity.

Bloom Season: Late spring and midsummer

Habitat/Range: Variable; found in rocky outcrops and scree slopes, moist or dry meadows or along streambanks from British Columbia to northern California.

Comments: *Delphinium* is from the Greek word *delphis* ("dolphin") and refers to the shape of the flower buds. *Menziesii* honors Archibald Menzies (1754–1842), a Scottish naval surgeon and botanist who sailed with Captain Vancouver on his 1790–1795 Pacific exploration. Plants contain a toxic alkaloid, delphinine, which diminishes with age.

157

PLAINS LARKSPUR
Delphinium nuttallium
Buttercup Family (Ranunculaceae)

Description: Perennial, stems upright to 20" from extensive fibrous roots. Leaves variable, borne on long stems the blades are highly divided. Flowers have 5 blue sepals and the upper 1 forms a spur. The petals are smaller and white. Fruit is a capsule.

Bloom Season: Spring

Habitat/Range: Drier sites in sagebrush flats, woodlands, and mountain slopes from British Columbia to California and east to Nebraska.

Comments: *Delphinium* is from the Greek word *delphis* ("dolphin") and refers to the shape of the flower buds. *Nuttallium* is for Thomas Nuttall (1786–1839), an English naturalist who collected plants and birds in the United States from 1811 to 1834. Bee pollinated.

BLUE BLOSSOM
Ceanothus thrysiflorus
Buckthorn Family (Rhamnaceae)

Description: Perennial shrub 3–20' tall. Egg-shaped leaves are 1–2" long, toothed along the margin and evergreen, and have 3 distinct veins running lengthwise. Blue flowers borne in dense clusters; each flower has 5 petals and stamens that protrude beyond the petals. Fruit is a capsule partitioned into 3 single-seeded sections.

Bloom Season: Mid spring to early summer

Habitat/Range: Coastal hills from western Washington to central California, and also the Columbia River Gorge.

Comments: *Ceanothus* is the Greek name for a spiny shrub, referring to certain members of this genus. *Thrysiflorus* ("flowers in a thyrse") reflects the type of floral arrangement: an elongated, narrowly branched cluster of flowers with blooms that mature from the bottom or outside towards the top or center of the cluster. In California this species may resemble a small tree growing to 25' in height with a 5–12" thick trunk. Also called California Lilac.

SMALL-FLOWERED BLUE-EYED MARY
Collinsia parviflora
Figwort Family (Scrophulariaceae)

Description: Annual, often low-growing but may be sprawling. Lower leaves stalked and spoon-shaped, while upper leaves stalkless and more lance-shaped. Flowers are ⅛–¼" long and 2-lipped. White upper lip is 2 lobed, while the deep blue lower lip is 3 lobed. Fruit is a tiny football-shape capsule bearing 4 smooth seeds with thick margins.

Bloom Season: Spring

Habitat/Range: Low to mid elevations in grassy fields, open areas, slopes, or rocky outcrops throughout the region. Native but considered weedy.

Comments: *Collinsia* is named for Zacheus Collins (1764–1831), an American botanist from Philadelphia. *Parviflora* ("small-flowered") describes the flowers. Often associated with the Virgin Mary because of their appearance around Easter.

WOODLAND PENSTEMON
Nothochelone nemorosa
Figwort Family (Scrophulariaceae)

Description: Perennial. From the woody base arise several tall stems up to 40". Leaves are arranged opposite each other along the stem, have short stems, and are lance to egg shaped. The leaf margins are sharply toothed. The tubular flowers are blue-purple or pink-purple and 2 lipped. The upper lip is shorter than the lower lip on the 1½"-long flowers. The stamens are very hairy on the tip. Fruit is a capsule.

Bloom Season: Early to midsummer

Habitat/Range: Woods and moist, rocky slopes from low to subalpine elevations.

Comments: *Nothochelone* refers to this plant being a false *Chelone,* which is another genus. *Chelone* ("turtle") refers to the front of the flower resembling a turtle's head, which is another common name.

BARRETT'S PENSTEMON
Penstemon barrettiae
Figwort Family (Scrophulariaceae)

Description: Perennial, spreading stems reach 6–16" long and create a matlike growth. The basal lance-shaped to elliptical leaves are 1½–5" long, borne on short stems, and may have spaced teeth along the margin; upper leaves are smaller. Both are bluish green and smooth. Rose-purple to lilac-colored flowers borne along one side of a flowering stalk; the 2-lipped flowers are 1–1½" long, keeled on the top, and 2 ridged on the inner lower lip with numerous white hairs inside. Fruit is a capsule.

Bloom Season: Late spring and early summer

Habitat/Range: Basalt cliffs and rocky slopes at low elevations in the eastern end of the Columbia River Gorge.

Comments: *Penstemon* is from *pen* ("almost") and *stemon* ("stamen"), which refers to the sterile stamen, called a staminoide, typical of this genus. *Barrettiae* is for Almeta Hodge Barrett, a doctor's wife living in Hood River, Oregon, who located the flower in the late 1800s. This penstemon has extensive root systems that penetrate deep within the rocky soil it inhabits. The leaves turn a striking purplish bronze in winter.

SHRUBBY PENSTEMON
Penstemon fruticosus
Figwort Family (Scrophulariaceae)

Description: Perennial, may be in dense colonies. Stems are prostrate and mat forming at the base, while the flowering stems rise 6–16". Leaves are evergreen, linear to inversely lance-shaped, and toothed along the margin. Corolla is blue-lavender to purplish and 1–2" long; flowers are arranged on 1 side of the flowering stem. The 2-ridged palate on the flower's lower lip has dense white or yellow hairs. Fruit is a capsule.

Bloom Season: Midspring to midsummer

Habitat/Range: Open rocky slopes to forests, foothills to mid elevation from British Columbia to Oregon and east into Idaho.

Comments: *Penstemon* is from *pen* ("almost") and *stemon* ("stamen"), which refers to the sterile stamen, called a staminoide, typical of this genus. *Fruticosus* ("shrubby or woody") refers to the stems. Separate varieties of this penstemon have slightly different leaves.

GLANDULAR PENSTEMON
Penstemon glandulosus
Figwort Family (Scrophulariaceae)

Description: Tall, robust perennial with stems to 40". Basal leaves large and triangular with soft hairs and sharply toothed margins. Both the basal and smaller upper stem leaves clasp the stem, as well as end with a tapered tip. The stout flowering stalks bear numerous flowers arranged in whorls; the buds are slightly sticky. The tubular, purplish blue flowers are 1–2" long and have 4 fertile stamens with barely noticeable short hairs on the anthers. Fruit is a capsule.

Bloom Season: Late spring to early summer

Habitat/Range: Open areas and forest edges in mid elevation sites from western Idaho to the foothills of the Cascades in central Washington to northern Oregon.

Comments: *Glandulosus* ("glandular") refers to the sticky hairs on the calyx. These large showy flowers attract hummingbirds, butterflies, and bees as pollinators. Also called Sticky-Stem Penstemon.

SMALL-FLOWERED PENSTEMON
Penstemon procerus
Figwort Family (Scrophulariaceae)

Description: Perennial with upright stems 4–24". The basal leaves form a loose cluster, have short stems, are up to 4" long, and are oval to lance shaped with smooth margins. The upper stem leaves are also opposite, but smaller and with toothed margins. The 2-lipped, bluish purple (occasionally tinged with pink) flowers are about ½" long and arranged in several whorls near the top of the stems and have a whitish throat. Fruit is a capsule.

Bloom Season: Late spring to summer

Habitat/Range: Dry sites in forests, meadows, and rocky areas in low to subalpine elevations from southern British Columbia to northern California and east into western Idaho.

Comments: *Penstemon* is from *pen* ("almost") and *stemon* ("stamen"), which refers to the sterile stamen, called a staminoide, typical of this genus. *Procerus* ("tall") refers to the upright stature of the plants. Bees and bumblebees squeeze between the open lips of the flower to access the nectar and pollen in the back.

COLUMBIA KITTENTAILS
Synthyris missurica
Figwort Family (Scrophulariaceae)

Description: Perennial, plants 6–16" tall. The long-stemmed, basal leaves are kidney shaped and 1–3" wide and have lobes or blunt teeth along the margins. Stem leaves are much smaller. The ¼"-long blue to purplish flowers are borne along an elongated stalk and have 4 petals of unequal length and 2 stamens that project beyond the flowers. Fruit is a rounded capsule.

Bloom Season: Spring to early summer

Habitat/Range: Shady woods or rocky slopes at low elevations from southeast Washington to northeast California and east to northern Idaho and Montana.

Comments: *Synthyris* ("fused doors") refers to the notched top of the capsule. *Missurica* ("of the Missouri River") describes the location where Meriwether Lewis collected a specimen in 1806. Also called Western Mountain Synthyris or Mountain Kittentails after the long spike of flowers resembling a kitten's tail.

EARLY BLUE VIOLET
Viola adunca
Violet Family (Violaceae)

Description: Perennial, but low-growing. Basal leaves are spear to heart shaped and have finely toothed margins. The upright stems bear long-stalked leaves, as well. From 1–5 floral stalks arise from the stems and bear a single, lavender-blue flower. The flowers are ¼–¾" wide and have 5 petals; the bottom petal is the largest and the spur is ½ the length of the lowest petal. The top of the style has hairs. Fruit is a capsule that bursts open at maturity.

Bloom Season: Spring

Habitat/Range: Moist meadows in mid to high elevations throughout North America.

Comments: *Viola* is the Latin name for various sweet-scented flowers, including violets. *Adunca* ("hooked") refers to the spur. Also called Hooked Violet or Western Dog Violet, this species is the state flower of Illinois, New Jersey, Rhode Island, and Wisconsin.

RED AND VIOLET FLOWERS

This section includes red and violet flowers as well as multicolored flowers that are predominantly red or violet. Since red and violet flowers often become either paler or deeper in color with age, you should check both the blue and purple and orange sections if you do not find the flower you are looking for in this section.

COLUMBIA DESERT PARSLEY
Lomatium columbianum
Carrot Family (Apiaceae)

Description: Perennial, mound-forming, usually less than 2' tall. The stems arise from a woody root. The highly dissected leaves are bluish green and have numerous linear leaflets. The flowering stalks bear an umbrella-like cluster of reddish purple flowers (rarely yellow). Fruit is a large seed with thick wings.

Bloom Season: Early spring

Habitat/Range: Rocky cliffs and canyon rims at low to mid elevations from the Columbia River Gorge north to central Washington.

Comments: *Lomatium* is from the Greek *loma* ("a border") and refers to the winged fruit. *Columbianum* ("of the Columbia River") refers to the location of the type specimen of these plants. The leaves feel very delicate.

SHOWY MILKWEED
Asclepias speciosa
Milkweed Family (Asclepiadaceae)

Description: Perennial, often growing in clusters, 2–3' tall. Large, thick oval leaves are up to 8" long, covered with fine white hairs and are arranged oppositely. A torn leaf or stem will bleed a white, milky latex. Flowers are borne in rounded clusters that hang from short, stout stalks. Star-shaped flowers have 5 rose-purple petals and 5 pinkish cream-colored, pouch-shaped hoods. Fruit is a spiny pod, 3–5" long.

Bloom Season: Summer

Habitat/Range: Disturbed areas and sandy sites and along waterways on the east side of the Cascades from British Columbia to California and east to the Mississippi Valley.

Comments: The genus *Asclepias* honors the Greek physician and god of medicine *Asklepios*. According to legend Asklepios boasted that he could revive the dead, which brought about retaliation from Hades (god of the underworld) and Zeus, who killed the physician with a lightning bolt. *Speciosa* ("showy") describes the flower heads. This species is the primary host plant for Monarch butterfly larvae.

ROSY PUSSYTOES
Antennaria microphylla
Sunflower Family (Asteraceae)

Description: Mat-forming perennial with horizontal runners and upright flowering stems from 2–19" tall. Basal leaves very hairy and paddle or lance shaped. Stem leaves smaller and narrow. Clusters of flower heads made up of only disk flowers. The involucre bracts are pinkish to white and about ¼" long. Fruit is a seed with white hairs.

Bloom Season: Late spring and summer

Habitat/Range: Widespread from grassy slopes and meadows in low to subalpine elevations throughout the region.

Comments: *Antennaria* is from the Latin *antenna* ("a ship's yard") either a horizontal pole that supports the sail or a mast used to hold signal flags, and this is also the derivation for an insect's antennae; hence, the genus name after the seed's white hairs which resemble butterfly antennae describes the flower heads that remain intact long after the growing season. *Microphylla* ("small leaved") refers to the leaf size. The common name refers to the resemblance of the flower heads to the underside of a cat's paw.

SPOTTED KNAPWEED
Centaurea bieberstenii
Sunflower Family (Asteraceae)

Description: Perennial, 1–3' tall. Numerous branches bear compound leaves divided into narrow segments. The flower heads bear pink-purple disk flowers. The bracts below the heads are arranged in several, overlapping rows and have dark, comblike tips. Fruit is a seed with white bristles on the tip.

Bloom Season: Mid spring through summer

Habitat/Range: Disturbed areas, fields, rangelands, and urban settings across the region.

Comments: *Centaurea* is from the Greek *kentauros* for the centaur Chiron, who used a similar plant for healing purposes. *Bieberstenii* is for Baron Friedrick August Marshall von Bieberstein, a 19th-century German who explored southern Russia. This Eurasian native is one of several weedy knapweeds that have invaded rangelands and urban areas in the United States. Knapweeds release a phytotoxin, catechin, from the roots. The toxin inhibits other plants from growing nearby. Knapweed produces abundant nectar to attract honeybees, butterflies, and other insects.

SEASIDE DAISY
Erigeron glaucus
Sunflower Family (Asteraceae)

Description: Perennial, with mostly mat-forming stems and a stout taproot. Basal leaves are thick, inversely lance to spatula shaped and toothed along the upper margins. Flowering heads have numerous pinkish to white ray flowers that surround a central cluster of yellow disk flowers. Heads are 1–2" wide. Fruit is a seed.

Bloom Season: Summer

Habitat/Range: Coastal bluffs, headlands, and rocky outcrops from Oregon to California.

Comments: *Erigeron* is from the Greek *eri* ("early") and *geron* ("old man") referring to the white hairs on the seeds. *Glaucus* ("white coating") refers to the leaves. The large flower surface attracts a variety of insects as pollinators in summer.

EUROPEAN SEAROCKET

Cakile maritima
Mustard Family (Brassicaceae)

Description: Perennial, with fleshy stems growing upright or sprawled across the sand. The 2–4" long leaves are also fleshy and deeply lobed. Pale pink flowers with 4 petals arise in sparse clusters and are about ½" wide. The fruits are an inflated silique with hornlike lobes.

Bloom Season: Summer

Habitat/Range: Coastal beaches from British Columbia to California. Introduced from Europe.

Comments: *Cakile* is from the old Arabic name for the plant. *Maritima* ("maritime") refers to the plant's distribution. American Searocket *(C. edentula)* has lobed or toothed leaves and lacks the hornlike projections on the fruit.

OAK TOOTHWORT

Cardamine pulcherrima
Mustard Family (Brassicaceae)

Description: Perennial, 3–10" tall. The stem leaves have 3–5 lobes; plants lack basal leaves. The flowers are borne in loose clusters at the top of the flowering stalk. The ½"-wide flowers are pale pink and have 4 petals with dark nectar lines. Fruit is a slender pod.

Bloom Season: Early spring

Habitat/Range: Shady woods, often associated with oaks, at low elevations from British Columbia to California on the west side of the Cascades.

Comments: *Cardamine* is the ancient Greek name for related plants. *Pulcherrima* ("very pretty") refers to the flowers. Pennsylvania Bitter-Cress *(C. pensylvanica)* is a related species that has a peppery flavor to its edible leaves.

DAGGER-POD
Phoenicaulis cheiranthoides
Mustard Family (Brassicaceae)

Description: Perennial, often with sprawling, reddish purple flowering stems. Basal leaves in cluster are grayish white, elliptical to inversely lance-shaped and 1–7" long. Flowering stalks are up to 8" long and bear reddish purple, pink, or white flowers. Flowers have 4 petals and are borne in dense clusters. Fruit is a daggerlike pod (shown in photo).

Bloom Season: Mid spring to early summer

Habitat/Range: Open, dry areas such as grasslands or sagebrush flats from low to mid elevations from eastern Washington to Oregon and east to Idaho.

Comments: *Phoenicaulis* is from *phoni* ("reddish purple") and *caulis* ("stem") in reference to the reddish stems. *Cheiranthoides* ("hand of flowers") refers to the different flowering stems spreading in different directions from the center.

OREGON BOXWOOD
Paxistima myrsinites
Staff-Tree Family (Celastraceae)

Description: Shrub, 10–40" tall with reddish brown branches. The evergreen leaves are opposite, oval to elliptical, ½–1½" long, and sharply toothed along the margin. The tiny reddish flowers are borne in small clusters in the leaf axils and have spreading petals. The 4 petals are borne on the outer rim of the floral disk. The fruit is a 1- or 2-seeded capsule covered with white.

Bloom Season: Early to mid spring

Habitat/Range: Coniferous forests at low to mid elevations from British Columbia to California and east to the Rocky Mountains.

Comments: *Paxistima* is from *pachys* ("thick") and *stigma* ("a stigma") after the thickened stigma. *Myrsinites* ("*Myrsine*like") refers to the plants' resemblance to myrtle. Oregon Boxwood is used extensively in the floral arranging industry. The genus may be spelled *Pachyistima,* and another common name is Mountain Lover.

CANDY STICK
Allotropa virgata
Heath Family (Ericaceae)

Description: Saprophyte, grows 5–18" tall. Stem is red with white stripes and bears whitish scalelike leaves. Flowers, borne at the top of the stalk, are urn shaped and reddish white and have 5 sepals and 10 stamens. Fruit is a capsule.

Bloom Season: Summer

Habitat/Range: Moist coniferous woodlands in humus at low elevations from British Columbia to California.

Comments: *Allotropa* is from the Greek *allos* ("other") and *tropos* ("to turn") in reference to the flowers, which are oriented around the stalk rather than on one side like the related Indian Pipe *(Monotropa uniflora)*. *Virgata* ("twiggy") refers to the stature of the plant. Look for crab spiders on the flowers, which capture unsuspecting pollinators.

KINNIKINNICK
Arctostaphylos uva-ursi
Heath Family (Ericaceae)

Description: Perennial, low-growing (up to 10" tall) with stems that mostly trail along the ground. Evergreen leaves are oval to spoon shaped and have entire margins. Urn-shaped flowers are pinkish white and ¼" long and hang downwards in clusters. Fruit is a red berry.

Bloom Season: Mid spring to midsummer

Habitat/Range: Widespread from low elevations to alpine areas often growing in sandy or rocky sites in clearings or forests.

Comments: *Arctostaphylos* is from the Greek *arktos* ("a bear") and *staphyle* ("a bunch of grapes"), which refers to the abundant fruits. *Uva-ursi* ("bear's grape") also refers to these fruits. Pinemat Manzanita *(A. nevadensis)* grows in the Oregon Cascades and southern Washington and has brownish red berries. Native tribes collected and dried Kinnikinnick leaves for smoking, often adding it to tobacco. The mealy berries were collected and eaten as well.

BOG LAUREL
Kalmia microphylla
Heath Family (Ericaceae)

Description: Shrub with multiple, low-growing stems, but may reach 2–3' tall. Alternate to whorled evergreen leaves are elliptical to inversely lance-shaped, ½–1" long with edges that may or may not roll inwards. Pale pink flowers borne in terminal clusters are saucer shaped and ½–1" wide and have 5 lobes. Ten stamens are evenly spaced around the lobes. Fruit is a 5-celled capsule.

Bloom Season: Blooms in summer

Habitat/Range: Wet areas in bogs, swamps, streambanks, and meadows from low to alpine elevations from Alaska to California and east to Colorado.

Comments: *Kalmia* is for Peter Kahm (1715–1779), a student of Carl Linnaeus. *Microphylla* ("small leaves") describes the stature of the leaves. Each stamen's anther is tucked into a pocket in the petal lobe and is held there under tension like a bent toothpick. A foraging insect trips the stamen's filament and the anther pops up and dusts the insect's underbelly with pollen. The plant contains a toxic glycoside called grayanotoxin; if ingested, it may cause nausea, vomiting, dizziness, breathing difficulties, and decreased blood pressure. Also known as Alpine Laurel or Western Swamp Laurel.

PINK MOUNTAIN-HEATHER
Phyllodoce empetriformis
Heath Family (Ericaceae)

Description: Shrub, often mat-forming, with stems 4–18" tall. Needlelike leaves are evergreen, numerous and ½" long. Bell-shaped pink to red flowers are borne in small clusters, and the flowers have 5 sepals and are ⅓" long. Flowers may be erect or hanging down. Fruit is a round capsule.

Bloom Season: Summer

Habitat/Range: Moist meadows and open forests in subalpine to alpine areas throughout the region.

Comments: *Phyllodoce* is after the Greek sea-nymph Phyllodoce, as Linnaeus started the custom of naming genera in the Heath Family after goddesses and sea nymphs. *Empetriformis* ("*Empetrum*-like") refers to the leaves resembling those of the Crowberry *(Empetrum nigrum)*. White Mountain-Heather *(Cassiope mertensiana)* has white, bell-shaped flowers.

PINK WINTERGREEN
Pyrola asarifolia
Heath Family (Ericaceae)

Description: Perennial, 2–14" tall. The basal cluster of leaves is glossy green, evergreen, long stalked, and rounded. The upright, reddish floral stem bears numerous pink, cup-shaped flowers that have waxy petals. Fruit is a capsule.

Bloom Season: Summer

Habitat/Range: Moist sites in forests at low to subalpine elevations throughout most of North America.

Comments: *Pyrola* ("pearlike") refers to the pearlike leaves. *Asarifolia* ("*Asarum*like leaves") refers to the similarity of the leaves to those of Wild Ginger. The undersides of the leaves may be pink, hence, the common name.

PACIFIC RHODODENDRON
Rhododendron macrophyllum
Heath Family (Ericaceae)

Description: Shrub, up to 24' tall. The alternate, leathery leaves are evergreen, elliptical, and 4–10" long. Clusters of bell-shaped, rose-purple flowers are borne at the ends of branches. The flowers are 1–2" long with 5 wavy lobes. The fruit is a capsule.

Bloom Season: Mid spring

Habitat/Range: Coniferous or mixed woodlands with acidic soils at sea level to mid elevations from southern British Columbia to northern California.

Comments: *Rhododendron* is from *rhodon* ("a rose") and *dendron* ("tree") after the colorful blossoms growing on sizeable shrubs. *Macrophyllum* ("large-leaved") describes the leaf size. Rhododendrons contain a toxic glycoside, andromedotoxin, which if concentrated in honeybee hives can cause poisoning to those that consume the honey. This is the state flower of Washington.

BLACK HUCKLEBERRY
Vaccinium membranaceum
Heath Family (Ericaceae)

Description: Shrub, 2–6' tall. The thin leaves are egg shaped to elliptical, 1–2½" long, and pointed at the tip and have small teeth along the margin. The small, urn-shaped flowers hang downwards and have 5 petals. Fruit is firm blackish purple berry (photo).

Bloom Season: Early summer

Habitat/Range: Open forests at mid to subalpine elevations from British Columbia to California (Olympic and Cascade Mountains) and east into Idaho.

Comments: *Vaccinium* is the Latin name for blueberries or huckleberries. *Membranaceum* ("thin or membranous") refers to the leaves. The edible fruits were, and still are, prized by Northwest inhabitants, including wildlife.

EVERGREEN HUCKLEBERRY
Vaccinium ovatum
Heath Family (Ericaceae)

Description: Shrub, 1–13' tall, with very leafy stems. The evergreen leaves are egg to broadly lance shaped, 1–2½" long, and finely toothed along the margin. The flowers arise from the leaf axils in clusters of 3–10. The ¼"-long, narrowly rounded flowers are pinkish. Fruit is a small, rounded purplish black berry.

Bloom Season: Mid to late spring

Habitat/Range: From the coast to the west side of the Cascades at low to mid elevations from British Columbia to northwest California.

Comments: *Vaccinium* is a Latin name for blueberries or huckleberries. *Ovatum* ("egg-shaped") refers to the leaves. The edible fruits were harvested by coastal tribes and either eaten fresh, or dried and baked into heavy breads, some weighing 10–15 pounds. Meriwether Lewis commented that the shrub retained its character during the winter.

WOOLLY-POD MILKVETCH
Astragalus purshii
Pea Family (Fabaceae)

Description: Perennial, low-growing, 2–6" tall. Compound basal leaves are woolly and bear 7–19 paired leaflets. The leaflets are elliptical and pointed at the tip. The pinkish, pea-shaped flowers may be white, yellow, or purplish. Flowers have a long tube that flares to a 2-lipped opening. Fruit is a woolly, ½–1" long seedpod.

Bloom Season: Spring

Habitat/Range: Dry sites in grasslands and sagebrush flats at low elevations from southern British Columbia to northern California and east to Montana and New Mexico.

Comments: *Astragalus* may be from the Greek *astragulos* ("ankle bone") referring to the shape of the pods. *Purshii* honors Frederick Traugott Pursh (1774–1820), a German botanist who worked on the Lewis and Clark plant collection and wrote *Flora Americae Septentrionalis,* a flora of North America, in 1814.

FEW-FLOWERED PEA
Lathyrus pauciflorus
Pea Family (Fabaceae)

Description: Perennial with upright stems, 2–3'
tall. Compound leaves have 8–10 egg-shaped
leaflets and are in pairs. Tendrils arise at the leaf
tip. The lavender to purple pea-shaped flowers
turn blue with age. The fruit is a pod.

Bloom Season: Spring

Habitat/Range: Drier sites in woodlands,
meadows, and sagebrush flats at low to mid
elevations from eastern Washington to California
and east to Idaho and Arizona.

Comments: *Lathyrus* is from the Greek name for
peas—*lathyros*. *Pauciflorus* is from the Latin
pauci ("few") and *florus* ("flowers") in reference
to the few flowers per stem. Pollinated by
bumblebees.

BIG-HEAD CLOVER
Trifolium macrocephalum
Pea Family (Fabaceae)

Description: Perennial, mostly low-growing
although plants might reach 10–12" high.
Compound leaves have 5–7 (sometimes 9) hairy
leaflets, that arise from a common point, with
fine-toothed edges. Tiny white, cream, pink, or
rose-colored flowers are arranged in dense, 2"-
wide rounded clusters. Clusters may contain up to
60 flowers. Fruit is a 1-seeded pod.

Bloom Season: Spring

Habitat/Range: Abundant in dry, rocky sites in
sagebrush plains and Ponderosa Pine woodlands
on the east side of the Cascades from Washington
to California and east into Idaho and Nevada.

Comments: *Trifolium* ("3 leaves") is a name given
to species in this genus that have 3 leaflets, and
macrocephalum ("large head") refers to the large
flower clusters. This is a native clover species
that attracts numerous bees, wasps, and flies as
pollinators.

SAND CLOVER
Trifolium wildenowii
Pea Family (Fabaceae)

Description: Annual, with matlike clusters. Compound leaves have 3 linear, sharp-pointed leaflets; the leaflets are about ½" long. Flower heads have a saucer-shaped bract with a spiny margin below the ½–1½" wide flowering heads. Heads contain up to 60 pink to purplish flowers with white tips. Fruit is a pod.

Bloom Season: Early spring

Habitat/Range: Grassy hillsides and meadows generally along the west side of the Cascades from British Columbia to California.

Comments: *Trifolium* ("3 leaves") is a name given to certain species in this genus that have 3 leaflets. *Wildenowii* is for Carl Ludwig Willdenow (1765–1812), a German botanist who was director of the Berlin Botanical Garden. The Scottish plant collector David Douglas recorded this plant in 1827 along the Columbia River. Also called Tomcat Clover.

SPRINGBANK CLOVER
Trifolium wormskjoldii
Pea Family (Fabaceae)

Description: Perennial, low-growing stems generally trail along the ground. The compound leaves are made up of 3 elliptical to inversely lance-shaped leaflets and may be greenish purple in color. Each leaflet is finely toothed along the margin and pointed at the tip. Clusters of bracts below the flower head are also toothed along the margin. White, pink, or reddish pea-shaped flowers are arranged in a dense cluster that may be ½–1" wide. Individual flowers often have white tips. Fruit is a pod with 1–4 seeds.

Bloom Season: Mid spring to fall

Habitat/Range: Moist, open ground along the coast or up into the mountains from British Columbia to Mexico and east into Idaho and New Mexico.

Comments: *Trifolium* ("3 leaves") refers to the leaflets of certain species in this genus. Also known as Cow Clover or Wormskjold's Clover. *Wormskjoldii* honors Morton Wormskjold (1783–1845), a Danish botanist who led an expedition to Greenland and who sailed with Kotzebue on his Pacific expedition. Coastal tribes harvested the roots in fall as a food source. An abundance of nectar attracts bees as pollinators.

AMERICAN VETCH
Vicia americana
Pea Family (Fabaceae)

Description: Perennial, stems sprawl along the ground or climb other plants. Compound leaves made up of 8–16 elliptical to linear leaflets with a tendril at the tip of the leaf. Small clusters of 3–9 pea-shaped, pinkish purple or bluish purple flowers arise on smooth flowering stalks. The style has a tuft of hairs at its tip. Fruit is a smooth pod.

Bloom Season: Mid spring to midsummer

Habitat/Range: Widespread in fields and deciduous or mixed woodlands from low to mid elevations throughout much of North America.

Comments: *Vicia* is derived from the Latin *vincio* ("to bind") and refers to the twinning nature of the plant. *Americana* ("from America") refers to the native distribution of this vetch. The leaves are highly variable for this native vetch.

GIANT VETCH
Vicia nigricans
Pea Family (Fabaceae)

Description: Perennial, sprawling; stems to 6' long. Compound leaves have 16–30 leaflets that are broadly lance-shaped. Tendrils enable the plant to trellis up vegetation. The pea-shaped flowers are borne in dense clusters, are 1" long, and bronze to reddish purple. Fruit is a seedpod.

Bloom Season: Mid spring through summer

Habitat/Range: Beaches, streambanks, or clearings along the coast from Alaska to California and inland to the Willamette Valley.

Comments: *Vicia* is derived from the Latin *vincio* ("to bind") and refers to the twinning nature of the plant. *Nigricans* ("blackish") refers to the roots. Bee pollinated.

WESTERN CORYDALIS
Corydalis scouleri
Bleeding Heart Family (Fumariaceae)

Description: Perennial, often in dense clusters, with stems 2–4' tall. The compound leaves divide 2–4 times and the leaflets are oval- or lance-shaped and 1–2½" long. The pinkish (white to rose to purplish) flowers are borne in a tight cluster along an elongated stalk and face one direction. The 4-petaled flowers are borne on short stems attached to their middle. The upper petal forms a hood and long spur, while the lower petal flares at the mouth. The side petals have crests. Fruit is a capsule.

Bloom Season: Mid spring to midsummer

Habitat/Range: Moist, shady woods from low to high elevations on the west side of the Cascades from southern British Columbia to northern Oregon.

Comments: *Corydalis* ("a lark") refers to the resemblance of the floral spur to that of the lark. *Scouleri* is for John Scouler (1804–1871), a Scotsman who joined the British Navy as a surgeon and who botanized with David Douglas in the Northwest. The flower's spur contains nectar that bumblebees seek, landing on the lateral petals joined together at their tips. This forces the upper petal apart and dusts the bees with pollen.

WILD BLEEDING HEART
Dicentra formosa
Bleeding Heart Family (Fumariaceae)

Description: Perennial, spreading by underground roots. The stout stems are 8–20" tall and bear basal compound leaves on long stems that are fernlike—highly dissected and lobed. The flowering stalk bears 4–15 pinkish (sometimes white), heart-shaped flowers that hang downwards. Of the 4 petals, the outer 2 have short spurs that spread outwards. Fruit is a podlike capsule with black seeds.

Bloom Season: Late spring and summer

Habitat/Range: Moist sites in woodlands and along streams from low to mid elevations from British Columbia to central California.

Comments: *Dicentra* is from the Greek *dis* ("twice") and *kentron* ("a spur") after the 2 spurs formed by the petals. *Formosa* ("beautiful") describes the flower. The seed tips have a tiny white appendage that is rich in oil and is coveted by ants. The ants carry the seeds to their nest acting as dispersal agents for the seeds. Hummingbirds pollinate the flowers.

RED CURRANT
Ribes sanguineum
Gooseberry Family (Grossulariaceae)

Description: Shrub, with woody, spineless stems that are 3–15' tall. The rough leaves have 3–5 shallow lobes, are 1–4" long, and have minute teeth along the edges. Tubular flowers are borne in clusters of 10–30 pale to deep pink flowers that hang down. The 5 sepals flare outwards forming a star-shaped pattern about ½" wide. The smaller white to red petals form a short tube that projects beyond this star-pattern. Fruit is a black berry.

Bloom Season: Early summer

Habitat/Range: Variable, moist, or dry woodlands or valleys from sea level to mid elevations from British Columbia to California and on the east slope of the Cascades in Washington and Oregon.

Comments: *Ribes* is from the Arabic or Persian *ribas* ("acid-tasting"), which refers to the fruits of some species. *Sanguineum* ("blood red") refers to the color of the flowers. Hummingbirds, bees, and butterflies pollinate the flowers. The flowers may appear before the leaves in the early spring. Red Currant is a host to White Pine Blister Rust *(Cronartium ribicola)*, a fungus with a life cycle that includes this currant and Western White Pine *(Pinus monticola)*. This species does well in cultivated gardens.

GRASS WIDOWS
Olsynium douglasii
Iris Family (Iridaceae)

Description: Perennial, plants 6–10" tall. Two grasslike leaves arise from the base. The reddish to lavender flowers are about 1" wide and have 6 tepals with white bases. Fruit is a capsule.

Bloom Season: Early spring

Habitat/Range: Meadows, grasslands, and open forests from low to mid elevations from British Columbia to California, mainly west of the Cascades.

Comments: The derivation of *Olsynium* is unclear. *Douglasii* is for the Scotsman David Douglas (1798–1834), who collected plants in the Northwest for the Horticultural Society of London. Another Grass Widow *(O. inflatum)* is similar but occurs farther east into Idaho and Utah, and the pistil is more inflated.

COOLEY'S HEDGE-NETTLE
Stachys chamissonis
Mint Family (Laminaceae)

Description: Perennial, 3–6' tall with square, unbranched stems with bristlelike hairs. The leaves are 3–7" long, opposite, triangular to heart-shaped in outline, and toothed along the margin. Flowers are borne in clusters along the upper portion of the stem. Green sepals are fused into a short tube with 5 spine-tipped lobes. The reddish purple petals are fused into an upper and lower, 3-lobed lip. Fruits are 4 small nutlets.

Bloom Season: Summer

Habitat/Range: Moist sites in clearings, wetlands, swamps, and forest edges or openings at low elevations from southern British Columbia to Oregon.

Comments: *Stachys* is Greek for ("spike") in reference to the flower arrangement, and *chamissonis* is after the French-born German botanist Adelbert von Chamisso (1781–1838), who collected plants in California in 1816. The common name is for Grace Cooley, a New Jersey professor of botany who first identified this plant in 1891. The growth form of this plant resembles Stinging Nettle *(Urtica dioica);* hence, the common name. The crushed stems have an unpleasant, versus minty, odor.

HOOKER'S ONION
Allium acuminatum
Lily Family (Liliaceae)

Description: Perennial from a bulb; grows 6–17" tall. The 1 or 2 grasslike leaves wither before the flower blooms. The floral stalk bears a cluster of pink or rose-purple flowers (occasionally white). The majority of the flowers are upright, not hanging downward, and the sepals have pointed tips that curl slightly backwards. Two papery bracts sit below the flower cluster. Fruit is a capsule.

Bloom Season: Mid spring to early summer

Habitat/Range: Dry rocky or sandy sites, open hillsides, or low elevation forests across the region from Vancouver Island to California and east to western Colorado.

Comments: *Allium* is from the Greek name for garlic, and *acuminatum* ("pointed") refers to the pointed sepal tips. The common name honors Sir William Jackson Hooker (1785–1865), a British botanist who named and catalogued hundreds of plant specimens collected by Northwest plant collectors in the 19th century. Nodding Onion *(A. cernuum)* has pinkish flowers arranged in a "nodding" cluster.

BALL-HEAD CLUSTER LILY
Dichelostemma congesta
Lily Family (Liliaceae)

Description: Perennial that grows 1–5' tall. Leaves are long, rounded, and linear and often wither prior to flowering. Flowering stalks bear a cluster of light to dark purple, 6-sepaled flowers. Flower clusters are ball shaped and may be over 2" wide. Fruit is a capsule.

Bloom Season: Mid spring to early summer

Habitat/Range: Dry meadows, rocky fields, sagebrush slopes, and grassy areas in Oregon and Washington.

Comments: *Dichelostemma* is from the Greek *dicha* ("bifid") and *stemma* ("a garland"), which refers to the forked ends on the sterile stamens. *Congesta* ("congested") refers to the dense floral cluster. Coastal natives ate the starchy bulbs. Also called Ookow, these lilies often grow in abundance.

PURPLE LOOSESTRIFE
Lythrum salicaria
Loosestrife Family (Lythraceae)

Description: Perennial, plants are 2–10' tall. The opposite leaves are 1½–5" long and lance-shaped with heart-shaped leaf bases. Reddish purple flowers are borne along an elongated stalk. The 5–7 petals are about ½" long and are paddle shaped. Fruit is a capsule.

Bloom Season: Mid to late summer

Habitat/Range: Marshes or wet areas throughout the region. Introduced from Europe, this loosestrife is considered a noxious weed.

Comments: *Lythrum* is from the Greek *luthron* ("blood") and refers to the color of the flowers. *Salicaria* ("willowlike") refers to the leaves. This European species was used medicinally to treat dysentery, diarrhea, fevers, cholera, and liver problems. Widespread in the United States; imported beetles from Europe *(Galerucella calmariensis* and *G. pusilla)* are used as bio-controls to limit growth.

FIREWEED
Chamerion angustifolium
Evening Primrose Family (Onagraceae)

Description: Perennial. Stems may grow 2–9' tall and are often unbranched. The stalkless leaves are lance-shaped and 2–10" long. Clusters of flowers arise at the ends of the stems. The rose to reddish purple flowers are 1–2" wide with 4 petals and a 4-lobed stigma. The long podlike capsule splits open to release numerous white-haired seeds.

Bloom Season: Midsummer to fall

Habitat/Range: Disturbed sites such as clearings, burns, meadows, avalanche paths, and roadsides from low to high elevations throughout the region.

Comments: *Chamerion* is from the Greek *chamae* ("lowly") and *nerion* ("Oleander") referring to the plants resemblance to a low-growing Oleander. *Angustifolium* ("having narrow leaves") indicates the lance-shaped leaves. The common name describes the habit of this plant colonizing recently burned areas. After the 1980 Mount St. Helens eruption, Fireweed was one of the first plants to sprout in the area. The upright spikes of flowers attract bees that visit the older, lower flowers first before moving up to higher flowers.

RAGGED ROBINS
Clarkia pulchella
Evening Primrose Family (Onagraceae)

Description: Annual, 4–20" tall but some are up to 3'. Linear leaves arranged alternately along the stem. Lavender to rose-purple flowers have 4 petals that are more or less 3-lobed at the tip and narrow (clawed) at the base. Two sets of stamens may be present, with one set being fertile and the other infertile and smaller. Fruit is a slender capsule.

Bloom Season: Late spring to early summer

Habitat/Range: Grows in dry grasslands, meadows, or open woods from British Columbia to Oregon and Idaho, east of the Cascades.

Comments: Frederick Pursh, the botanist charged with identifying specimens from the Lewis and Clark Expedition, named the genus after William Clark (1770–1838). *Pulchella* ("pretty") refers to the lovely flowers. Meriwether Lewis first recorded this plant on June 1, 1806: "I met with a singular plant today in blume of which I preserved a specemine . . . " is how Lewis began his description of this plant. Also known as Elkhorns, Deer Horn, or Beautiful Clarkia.

FAIRY-SLIPPER
Calypso bulbosa
Orchid Family (Orchidaceae)

Description: Perennial, growing from a marble-sized bulb. A single flowering stem arises 4–8" from the bulb. The single oval-shaped leaf often fades during the summer. The 1" long flower varies from pink to rose-purple in color (sometimes white or cream). A single inflated petal forms the "slipper" portion of the flower and bears 2 hornlike projections at the base. This petal has purplish spots and streaks. Above this petal is the hood, which cloaks the stamens and styles. Above the hood are 2 more petals and 3 sepals that are lance-shaped and project up and outwards. Fruit is a capsule.

Bloom Season: Late spring and early summer

Habitat/Range: Found throughout the Northwest in coniferous forests from sea level to high elevations, and occurs from Alaska throughout Canada and south to California, Colorado, and Arizona.

Comments: *Calypso* is named after the sea nymph *Kalypso,* which is from a Greek word meaning "covered or hidden." *Bulbosa* ("bulbous") refers to the swollen underground stem. These orchids are pollinated by inexperienced bees, which seek nectar rewards that the plants "advertise" through their fragrance and coloration. However, they produce no nectar for these pollinators; mature bees leave the flowers alone and the plants depend upon successive generations of inexperienced bees to continue the pollination process. Also called Deer Orchid.

SPOTTED CORALROOT
Corallorhiza maculata
Orchid Family (Orchidaceae)

Description: Saprophyte, often with numerous upright, yellowish red or brown stems, 8–18" tall. Plants lack green leaves but have small translucent scales along the stem. The pink or reddish (reddish orange) flowers are borne in a loose cluster at the top of the stem. There are 3 reddish sepals and 3 petals—the lower petal forms a white 3-lobed lip with several reddish spots. The other 2 petals are reddish and arch around and over the 3rd petal. Fruit is a capsule with numerous seeds.

Bloom Season: Late spring and summer

Habitat/Range: Grows in humus or forest duff at low to mid elevations across the region and North America.

Comments: *Corallorhiza* is from the Greek *korallion* ("coral") and *rhiza* ("root") and refers to the knobby coral-like roots. *Maculata* ("spotted") refers to the crimson spots on the flower. As saprophytes, these plants do not photosynthesize but obtain nutrients from soil fungi. The spotted lip offers a wide landing platform for insect pollinators such as flies or bees. As the insects search for nectar, they are dusted with pollen from stamens located in the upper hood of the flower. Stripped Coralroot *(C. striata)* has pinkish flowers with reddish brown or purple stripes.

WESTERN CORALROOT
Corallorhiza mertensiana
Orchid Family (Orchidaceae)

Description: Saprophyte, often with numerous upright reddish stems 8–20". The plants lack green leaves but have semitranslucent leaflike sheaths. The pink to reddish brown flowers are borne in a loose cluster at the top of the stem and have 3 slender sepals and 3 petals. The lower, pink to red lip lacks spots or stripes but may have a white tip. Two narrow sepals project outwards from the sides, while the 3rd sepal is fused to the 2 upper petals forming a hood. Fruit is a capsule with numerous seeds.

Bloom Season: Summer

Habitat/Range: Grows in humus or duff at low to mid elevations from Alaska to California and east to Montana and Wyoming. Sometimes found in close proximity to Spotted Coralroot *(C. maculata)*.

Comments: *Corallorhiza* is from the Greek *korallion* ("coral") and *rhiza* ("root") and refers to the knobby coral-like roots. *Mertensiana* is for Franz Carl Mertens (1764–1831), a professor of botany at Bremen. The knobby roots resemble coral; hence, the common name. As saprophytes, these plants do not photosynthesize but obtain nutrients from soil fungi. Similar to Spotted Coralroot, the wide lower lip provides a landing platform for insects that proceed into the flower in search of nectar. The insects are dusted with pollen from the stamens enclosed within the upper hood.

SEA THRIFT
Armeria maritima
Plumbago Family (Plumbaginaceae)

Description: Perennial, flowering stems up to 10". The linear basal leaves are stiff and spiny and form dense matlike clusters. Flowering stalks bear rounded clusters, ½–1½" wide, of tiny pink or lavender flowers. Papery bracts arise below the flower clusters, and the petals are also papery and may last on the plant long after the blooming season. Fruit is a single seed enclosed within a bladder that is often enclosed by the sepals.

Bloom Season: Mid spring to summer

Habitat/Range: Coastal bluffs and beaches, although possibly inland in grassy meadows. Sea Thrift has a circumboreal distribution.

Comments: *Armeria* is from the French name *armoires* ("cluster-headed dianthus"), which refers to a different, although similar, plant. *Maritima* ("coastal") refers to the plant's distribution. This species occurs in both coastal and inland horticultural gardens.

SCARLET GILIA
Ipomopsis aggregata
Phlox Family (Polemoniaceae)

Description: Biennial or short-lived perennial. One to several flowering stalks arise 1–3' from a basal rosette of highly dissected leaves. Stem leaves are smaller. Flowers are borne in loose clusters and are mostly red, although orange or yellow forms exist. Flowers have white to yellowish speckles, and the corolla tube flares open to form a 5-pointed star. Fruit is a capsule.

Bloom Season: Summer

Habitat/Range: Widespread in dry meadows, roadsides, rocky outcrops, or lightly wooded areas from low to high elevations east of the Cascades to Idaho and the Rocky Mountains.

Comments: *Ipomopsis* is from the Greek *ipo* ("to strike") and *opsis* ("resembling") in reference to the striking flowers. Gilia honors Felippo Luigi Gilii (1756–1821), an Italian astronomer and coauthor of *Osservazioni Fitologiche* (1789–92). *Aggregata* ("aggregated") refers to the cluster of basal leaves. Hummingbirds, butterflies, and certain moths are the primary pollinators that can reach the flower's nectar. Also called Skyrocket Gilia.

SPREADING PHLOX
Phlox diffusa
Phlox Family (Polemoniaceae)

Description: Perennial with low, matted growth. Numerous needlelike yellowish green leaves, opposite, ¼–¾" long, and sharply pointed. The flowers are ½–¾" wide and trumpet shaped and vary in color from pink to white to bluish. The 5 petals are fused together for most of their length. Fruit is a small capsule.

Bloom Season: Spring to late summer

Habitat/Range: Dry, open sites that are rocky or in woodlands from mid to higher elevations from British Columbia to California and east to western Montana.

Comments: *Phlox* ("flame") refers to the flower color and *diffusa* ("spreading") describes the plants' spreading nature. These plants often form a quiltlike pattern of flowers against a spring hillside attracting a number of early season pollinators.

LONG-LEAF PHLOX
Phlox longifolia
Phlox Family (Polemoniaceae)

Description: Perennial, 4–16" tall. Linear leaves are 1–3" long and opposite and have pointed ends. Trumpet-shaped pinkish (sometimes white) flowers are borne in clusters, and the 5 petals form a long tube that flares at the tip. The center collar is white, and the style is longer than the stamens. Fruit is a capsule.

Bloom Season: Mid spring to midsummer

Habitat/Range: Dry, open sites in sagebrush or shrublands at low to mid elevations, but may occur at higher elevations in the mountains. Widespread east of the Cascades.

Comments: *Phlox* ("flame") refers to the flower color and *longifolia* ("long leaves") describes the leaf length. Pollinators, such as butterflies or hummingbirds, need to have a long proboscis to reach the nectar rewards deep in the flower's tube. Showy Phlox *(P. speciosa)* is similar but with notched tips on the petal lobes and styles about the length of the stamens.

SHEEP SORREL
Rumex acetosella
Buckwheat Family (Polygonaceae)

Description: Perennial, up to 12" tall. The arrowhead-shaped leaves have flaring lobes near the base. The tiny reddish brown flowers are borne along an elongated stalk. Male and female flowers are on different plants. Fruit is a reddish-brown winged seed.

Bloom Season: Spring to summer

Habitat/Range: Widespread weedy species from low to subalpine elevations throughout the region.

Comments: *Rumex* is the Latin name for sorrel or dock. *Acetosella* is from the Latin *acetum* ("vinegar") in reference to the slightly bitter taste, due to oxalic acid, of the edible leaves. Mountain Sorrel *(Oxyria digyna)* is another sorrel with edible leaves, but this species has heart- to kidney-shaped leaves and grows in alpine areas.

SAND DOCK
Rumex venosus
Buckwheat Family (Polygonaceae)

Description: Perennial, spreads by thick roots. The upright stems are about 12" long and have broad, leathery leaves (up to 6" long) that are heavily veined. The flowers are borne in dense clusters; the inner parts are bright red. Fruits are bright red, 3-sided seeds.

Bloom Season: Spring to early summer

Habitat/Range: Sandy or rocky areas in grasslands or sagebrush flats at low elevations on the east side of the Cascades from British Columbia to California and east to the Dakotas.

Comments: *Rumex* is the Latin name for sorrel or dock. *Venosus* ("with prominent veins") refers to the leaves.

JEFFREY'S SHOOTING STAR
Dodecatheon jeffreyi
Primrose Family (Primulaceae)

Description: Perennial, up to 20" tall, with a stem that is up to ¼" thick. Leaves variable, inversely lance or spatula shaped, 4–7" long, and smooth or with glandular hairs. Flowering stalks may bear numerous flowers. The flowers are ½–1" long and have 4 or 5 pink to purple petals ringed with white and a red or purple base. Stamen filaments are dark. Fruit is a capsule.

Bloom Season: Late spring to early summer

Habitat/Range: Moist meadows and marshes in the mountains from Alaska to the California and east to Idaho.

Comments: *Dodecatheon* is from the Greek *dodeka* ("12") and *theos* ("god") meaning that the 12 Olympian gods protected the plants. *Jeffreyi* honors John Jeffrey (1826–1854), a gardener at the Edinburgh Botanical Garden in England. Bees pollinate the flowers. Also called Tall Mountain Shooting Star.

POET'S SHOOTING STAR
Dodecatheon poeticum
Primrose Family (Primulaceae)

Description: Perennial, up to 1' tall. Leaves are variable, mostly spatula-shaped, from 1½–6" long, and covered with fine glandular hairs. Margins of leaves may be toothed or smooth. Star-shaped flowers have pink-purple to rose-colored petals that bend backwards and are ringed with yellow and a red base. The stamen filaments are purple and short. Fruit is a capsule.

Bloom Season: Late spring and early summer

Habitat/Range: Grassy slopes and woodlands that are moist in spring but become drier from central Washington to Columbia River Gorge.

Comments: *Dodecatheon* is from the Greek *dodeka* ("12") and *theos* ("god") meaning that the 12 Olympian gods protected the plants. Bumblebees pollinate these flowers by hanging upside down from the yellow ring and "buzzing" their wings. Pollen shakes loose and lands on the bee's belly from which the bee gleans the pollen into leg sacs. When the bee visits another flower, leftover pollen comes in contact with that flower's stigma to complete pollen transfer. Also called Narcissus Shooting Star.

RED COLUMBINE
Aquilegia formosa
Buttercup Family (Ranunculaceae)

Description: A striking plant growing to 3' tall, bearing leaves that are twice divided into 3s. The majority of them is basal. The red and yellow drooping flowers have 5 long spurs and a central cluster of yellowish stamens and styles that project beyond the flower's mouth. Seeds are tiny, numerous, and black.

Bloom Season: Summer

Habitat/Range: A variety of moist sites that may be open or partially shaded throughout the region.

Comments: *Aquilegia* ("eagle") refers to the talonlike spurs on the flowers, and *formosa* ("beautiful") refers to the flowers. The red flowers attract hummingbirds and butterflies, which use their long tongues or proboscises to reach the nectar at the bulbous base of the spurs. Does well in ornamental gardens.

OLD MAN'S WHISKERS
Geum triflorum
Rose Family (Rosaceae)

Description: Perennial, 4–20" tall. The basal leaves are fernlike and hairy. The 1"-long, vase-shaped flowers are arranged in groups of 3 and hang downward. The pink to yellow petals are hidden beneath 5 red sepals and curved bracts. Seeds have long hairy plumes.

Bloom Season: Late spring to midsummer

Habitat/Range: Rocky outcrops, grassy slopes, and seasonally moist meadows at low to mid elevations east of the Cascades throughout the region.

Comments: *Geum* is the classic Latin name for this genus. *Triflorum* ("3 flowers") refers to the floral clusters. First collected by Meriwether Lewis in 1806. As the seeds mature, the flower stems turn upward. The 2" feathery tails on the seeds, which resemble whiskers, promote wind dispersal. Also called Prairie Smoke.

NOOTKA ROSE
Rosa nutkana
Rose Family (Rosaceae)

Description: Shrub, averaging 3–5' in height. Stems may have prickles or large, recurved thorns that form in pairs mostly near the new developing leaves. The compound leaves have 5–9 egg-shaped to elliptical leaflets, ½–3½" long, with saw-toothed margins. Flowers borne singularly at the end of stem are up to 3½" wide, fragrant, and pink to rose colored. The sepals remain on the plant after the flower matures. Fruits (hips) are bright red and rounded.

Bloom Season: Spring to early summer

Habitat/Range: Open woodlands, woodland edges, or thickets from sea level to mid elevations from Alaska to northern California and east to the Rocky Mountains.

Comments: *Rosa* is the Latin name for a rose. *Nutkana* refers to the Nootka Sound in British Columbia where the type specimen is from. High in vitamin C, rose hips were eaten as a last resort against starvation. Nathaniel Wyeth, in 1832, wrote about encountering a native woman and her children: "They had no food but rose hips of which we made our supper." Teas or poultices were also made from the branches or leaves for treating eye problems or sores. The Peafruit Rose *(R. pisocarpa)* also has thorns that occur near the leaf buds, but has smaller (up to 1½" wide), clustered flowers, and pointed leaflets and occurs in wet locations. The fragrant flowers attract bees, beetles, butterflies, and other pollinators.

WOODS' ROSE
Rosa woodsii
Rose Family (Rosaceae)

Description: Shrub, up to 3½' tall. Stems bear small prickles. Compound leaves have 5–9 egg-shaped to elliptical leaflets that are ½–1½" long and toothed along the margins. The 1–2" wide pinkish flowers retain their sepals in fruit. Fruit is a red rose hip.

Bloom Season: Summer

Habitat/Range: Along streams and forest edges from low to high elevations throughout the region.

Comments: *Rosa* is the Latin name for a rose. *Gymnocarpa* ("naked fruit") refers to the sepal-less smooth fruits. Flowers attract numerous bees, wasps, butterflies, and beetles as pollinators. Ballhip Rose *(R. gynocarpa)* has small flowers and fruits that lose their sepals.

DOUGLAS' SPIRAEA
Spiraea douglasii
Rose Family (Rosaceae)

Description: Shrub, 2–7' tall with numerous, upright branches. The deciduous leaves are 2–4" long, are toothed along the edge (from the middle to the tip) and have dense wool-like gray hairs on the undersides. Tiny flowers are arranged in dense, elongated clusters (several times longer than broad) that reach 2–6" long. The pink to rose-colored flowers fade with age. Fruit is a long pod.

Bloom Season: Summer

Habitat/Range: Moist locations along streams, rivers, meadows, and lakes from low to mid elevations from southern Alaska to northern California and east to central Idaho.

Comments: *Spiraea* is from the Greek *speiraira* ("a plant used for garlands"), while *douglasii* honors David Douglas (1798–1834), the Scottish botanist who collected plants in the Pacific Northwest for the Royal Horticultural Society in the mid 1820s. Look for bumblebees and butterflies sipping nectar on these flowers. Like Subalpine Spirea, the protruding stamens give the flowers a "fuzzy" appearance.

SUBALPINE SPIRAEA
Spiraea splendens
Rose Family (Rosaceae)

Description: Shrub, spreads by underground roots and reaches 40" tall. The numerous branches have reddish brown bark. The egg-shaped to elliptical leaves are 1–2" long and toothed along the margin. The dense flowering heads are flat topped or rounded and bear numerous pinkish flowers with stamens extending past the petals. Fruit is a few-seeded pod.

Bloom Season: Summer

Habitat/Range: Open woodlands, forest edges, and disturbed areas such as avalanche chutes or clearings at mid to subalpine elevations from southern British Columbia to California and east to Idaho and parts of Montana and Wyoming.

Comments: *Spiraea* is from the Greek *speiraira* ("a plant used for garlands"). *Splendens* ("splendid") refers to the flower heads. The stamens protrude above the petals giving the flower heads a "fuzzy" appearance. The mass of flowers provides pollinators, such as bees, opportunities to visit numerous flowers without having to search for other plants.

APPLEGATE'S PAINTBRUSH
Castilleja applegatei
Figwort Family (Scrophulariaceae)

Description: Perennial, with sticky-haired stems, 4–24" tall. The variable leaves are linear (lower) and 3 lobed (upper) with wavy margins. The reddish bracts have 3–5 lobes and surround a spoutlike, tubular, green corolla. Fruit is a capsule.

Bloom Season: Summer

Habitat/Range: Rocky outcrops or open woods at mid elevations from Oregon to California and east to Idaho.

Comments: *Castilleja* is for Domingo Castillejo (1744–1793), a Spanish professor of botany. *Applegatei* honors Elmer Applegate (1867–1949), a student of Oregon flora. Cliff Paintbrush *(C. rupicola)* has highly divided leaves and reddish bracts. Hummingbirds pollinate both species.

COMMON RED PAINTBRUSH
Castilleja miniata
Figwort Family (Scrophulariaceae)

Description: Perennial, with stems 10–36" tall. The entire leaves are smooth and lance shaped with entire margins. The hairy reddish bracts are 3-lobed and surround a greenish corolla. Fruit is a capsule.

Bloom Season: Late spring to early fall

Habitat/Range: Moist open meadows or along streams from sea level to subalpine elevations throughout the region.

Comments: *Castilleja* is for Domingo Castillejo (1744–1793), a Spanish professor of botany. *Miniata* ("Saturn-red") is for the scarlet-red bracts. Elmer's Paintbrush *(C. elmeri)* also has entire leaves but the flowers are purplish red with sticky hairs. Hummingbirds pollinate the flowers.

ANNUAL INDIAN PAINTBRUSH
Castilleja minor
Figwort Family (Scrophulariaceae)

Description: Annual, with stems 4–32" tall. The stems have sticky hairs. The leaves are narrowly lance-shaped. The upper floral bracts are tipped with red, while the corollas are yellow. Fruit is a capsule.

Bloom Season: Summer and early fall

Habitat/Range: Moist sites in meadows, marshes, or alkaline flats at low elevations throughout the western United States.

Comments: *Castilleja* is for Domingo Castillejo (1744–1793), a Spanish professor of botany. *Minor* ("smaller") refers to the small galea or upper helmetlike portion of the flower. Pollinated by hummingbirds.

FOXGLOVE
Digitalis purpurea
Figwort Family (Scrophulariaceae)

Description: Perennial, stout stems reach 1–7' tall. Basal leaves borne on long stems are 7–20" long, egg to lance shaped, and finely toothed along the margins. Upper leaves smaller. The flowering stalk bears numerous tube-shaped flowers that flare open at the mouth, droop slightly downwards, and are 2–3" long. The flowers are white, pink, red, or purple (or intergrades of these colors) and have spots inside the lower lip. Fruit is an egg-shaped capsule.

Bloom Season: Late spring and summer

Habitat/Range: Widespread in disturbed areas such as roadways, fields, fallow meadows, and forest edges from low elevation. Introduced from Europe, this plant occurs throughout the Northwest.

Comments: *Digitalis* is from the Latin *digitus* ("finger") and refers to the flower's resemblance to a glove's finger. *Purpurea* ("purple") describes one flower color. Flowering stalks mature from the bottom up; therefore, bees search upward for pollen. Also known as Devil's Fingers or Dead Men's Bells. Plants produce the compound digitalin, which is made into digitalis, a potent heart medicine that is used today.

LEWIS' MONKEY-FLOWER

Mimulus lewisii
Figwort Family (Scrophulariaceae)

Description: Perennial, often growing in thick clusters. Stems are 15–45" tall and covered with soft, sticky hairs. The oval-shaped leaves clasp the stem and are arranged oppositely. The leaves are toothed along the margin. Trumpet-shaped, rose-red or pinkish flowers are 1½–2" long and 2 lipped. The lower lip has 2 yellowish, hairy ridges. Fruit is a capsule.

Bloom Season: Summer

Habitat/Range: Moist clearings, streambanks, and rocky seeps from mid to high elevations from British Columbia to California and east to Colorado.

Comments: *Mimulus* ("mime or clown") refers to the flower. The common and species name honors Meriwether Lewis, leader of the Corps of Discovery expedition from 1804–1806. Pollinated by bees. Also called Pink Monkey-Flower.

DWARF PURPLE MONKEY-FLOWER
Mimulus nanus
Figwort Family (Scrophulariaceae)

Description: Low-growing annual, reaches 4–5" in good growing sites. Leaves are lance to egg shaped and covered with soft, sticky hairs. The lavender to purplish flowers are ½–1¼" long, borne singular or in clusters, and 2-lipped. Upper lip has 2 lobes, while the lower lip has 3. The lower lip has 2 yellow ridges with purple spots. Fruit is a capsule.

Bloom Season: Summer

Habitat/Range: Sagebrush communities, open forests, and dry woodlands from low to mid elevations in central Washington to Montana and south to northern California.

Comments: *Mimulus* ("mime or clown") refers to the flower. *Nanus* ("dwarf") refers to the plant's stature.

ELEPHANTHEAD
Pedicularis groenlandica
Figwort Family (Scrophulariaceae)

Description: Perennial, may be 6–20" tall. Leaves are fernlike, 2–6" long, and toothed along the margins. Reddish purple unbranched stems bear dense clusters of flowers at the terminal end. Each small pinkish flower resembles an elephant's head. The upper petal is round, resembling the head, and then tapers to the long trunk. Three lower petals resemble the 2 large ears and lower mouth. Fruit is a curved capsule.

Bloom Season: Late spring and early summer

Habitat/Range: Wet meadows and streambanks at mid to high elevations across Canada and south throughout the Cascade Range and east to the Rocky Mountains.

Comments: *Pedicularis* ("of lice") refers to the belief that livestock grazing in fields of these plants would become infested with lice. *Groenlandica* ("of Greenland") refers to the type locality. Bumblebees pollinate these flowers by perching on the trunk and forcing their way into the flower. Little Elephant's Head *(P. attollens)* is a similar species that occurs at subalpine elevations but the trunk barely extends beyond the flower's throat. Mount Rainier Lousewort *(P. rainierensis)* is another member of this genus with yellow to cream-colored flowers that grows in subalpine areas around Mount Rainier.

PALMER'S PENSTEMON
Penstemon palmeri
Figwort Family (Scrophulariaceae)

Description: Perennial, stout stems 20–56" tall. Basal and lower stem leaves are egg shaped and up to 4" long with a short stalk. Upper leaves are triangular or heart shaped and clasp the stem. Leaf edges are smooth or toothed. Floral stalk bears large, tubular flowers that are 1–1½" long and have wide openings. The pink to lavender 2-lipped flowers have prominent purplish nectar lines on the lower lips and throat and have a bearded sterile stamen that protrudes beyond the flower opening. Fruit is a capsule.

Bloom Season: Summer

Habitat/Range: Roadsides and cultivated areas, sagebrush flats, and pine woodlands from low to mid elevation in Idaho and eastern Oregon.

Comments: *Palmeri* honors Edward Palmer (1831–1911), an avid plant collector in North and South America, with over 200 species named for him. Though mainly a Southwestern species, this penstemon has been seeded for highway beautification projects and cultivated gardens and is now naturalized in Idaho. Bumblebees muscle into the flowers to seek nectar and pollen using the nectar lines as guides.

ROCK PENSTEMON
Penstemon rupicola
Figwort Family (Scrophulariaceae)

Description: Perennial, growing in dense mats. Evergreen leaves are opposite, short stemmed, and egg shaped with finely toothed margins. Tubular flowers are 1–1½" long, pink to reddish purple, and 2 lipped. The upper lip has a keel on the outside, while the lower lip has 2 white-hairy ridges. The anthers have long, white hairs. Fruit is a capsule.

Bloom Season: Late spring to midsummer

Habitat/Range: Rocky outcrops and basalt cliffs from low to high elevations in the Cascades from southern Washington to northern California.

Comments: *Rupicola* ("rocky") refers to the habitat preference of this penstemon. Also known as Cliff Penstemon, this species has woolly anther sacs. Davidson's Penstemon *(P. davidsonii)* is another low-growing, mat-forming penstemon with purple to lavender flowers that grows in rock outcrops.

SEA BLUSH
Plectritis congesta
Valerian Family (Valerianaceae)

Description: Annual, 4–30" tall. The short-stalked basal leaves are egg or club shaped while the stem leaves are egg shaped and stalkless. Leaves vary from ½ to 2" long and are arranged oppositely along the stem. Floral stalks bear a rounded cluster of pink (occasionally white) flowers. The 5-lobed individual flowers are tube shaped and about ⅛" wide and have a short spur at the base. Fruit is a winged seed.

Bloom Season: Mid spring to early summer

Habitat/Range: Moist meadows, rocky slopes, and bluffs at low elevations that dry up in summer from Vancouver Island south to California from the Cascades west to the coast.

Comments: *Plectritis* ("plaited") refers to the interwoven flower arrangement, and *congesta* ("congested") also refers to this arrangement. These plants may bloom in profusion covering large areas.

ORANGE FLOWERS

This section includes orange flowers as well as multicolored flowers that are predominantly orange. Since orange flowers often become either paler or deeper in color with age, you should check both the yellow and red sections if you do not find the flower you are looking for in this section.

ORANGE BALSAM
Impatiens capensis
Balsam Family (Balsaminaceae)

Description: Perennial. The alternate leaves are elliptical to oval and toothed along the margins. The flowers are 1–2" long and orange or brown spotted. The horn-shaped flowers appear inflated, but there are 4 petals and 3 sepals, 1 of which forms a curved spur. Fruit is a capsule with several seeds.

Bloom Season: Summer

Habitat/Range: Moist areas along streams, rivers, and thickets at low to mid elevations from northwest Washington to the Columbia River Gorge in Oregon, but also in the eastern United States and Canada.

Comments: *Impatiens* ("impatient") refers to the dispersal mechanism of the seeds. When the ripe capsule is touched, the pods explode lengthwise and hurl the seeds. *Capensis* ("of the Cape of Good Hope, South Africa") refers to the resemblance of the flower to the outline of South Africa. The succulent stems were crushed and the juice applied to poison ivy rashes. Also called Touch-Me-Not after the exploding capsule.

TIGER LILY
Lilium columbianum
Lily Family (Liliaceae)

Description: Plants may be 1–4' tall with hairless (usually) slender stems. Lance-shaped leaves, 2–5" long, are arranged in several whorls of 6–9 leaves. Upper stem leaves variable. Showy orange flowers have red or purple spots near the center. The tepals curve backwards to expose the orange anthers. Fruit is barrel-shaped and contains numerous seeds.

Bloom Season: Summer

Habitat/Range: Low to subalpine elevations in meadows, clearings, or open forests from British Columbia to California and east to Nevada.

Comments: *Lilium* is from the Greek *leirion* ("a lily"). *Columbianum* ("Columbia River") refers to the area where this plant was first collected. The edible bulbs are peppery. Hummingbirds pollinate the flowers.

CALIFORNIA POPPY
Eschscholzia californica
Poppy Family (Papaveraceae)

Description: Perennial, plants 6–24" tall. The highly divided basal leaves have a bluish tint and a lacy appearance. The flowering stalks bear a single, yellow to orange bowl-shaped flower, with 4 delicate petals, that is ½–2" long. The flower sits on a distinct rim that becomes more noticeable in fruit. Fruit is a long, slender seedpod.

Bloom Season: Mid spring through fall

Habitat/Range: Grassy slopes, rock outcrops, and disturbed areas at low elevations west of the Cascades from southwest Washington to southern California.

Comments: Named after Johann Friedrich von Eschoscholz (1793–1831), an eminent German physician, botanist, and naturalist who completed 2 circumnavigations of the globe with the explorer Otto von Kotzebe in 1815–1818 and 1823–1826. *Californica* ("of California") refers to the location of the type specimen; this is also the California state flower. The flowers close at night or during cloudy days. Bees, wasps, and beetles may be observed pollinating the flowers. A widely used ornamental.

LARGE-FLOWERED COLLOMIA
Collomia grandiflora
Phlox Family (Polemoniaceae)

Description: Annual, stems up to 40". These plants may have one or many stems. The narrow leaves are up to 2" long and not divided. The 1"-long, funnel-shaped flowers are arranged in sticky clusters and are salmon, light red, yellow, or white in color. The flowers flare open to reveal (barely) the 5 stamens. Fruit is a capsule.

Bloom Season: Late spring and summer

Habitat/Range: Dry, open woodlands on either side of the Cascades from British Columbia to California and east to Montana.

Comments: *Collomia* is from the Greek *colla* ("glue") and refers to the stickiness of the wet seeds. *Grandiflora* ("large flower") refers to the flower's size. The leaves were steeped to make a soothing eyewash.

GREAT POLEMONIUM
Polemonium carneum
Phlox Family (Polemoniaceae)

Description: Perennial, sprawling stems up to 15–50" long. The compound basal leaves have numerous elliptical leaflets. Salmon to whitish or blue flowers are borne in dense clusters. The funnel-shaped flowers are about 1" wide and have 5 petals. Fruit is a capsule.

Bloom Season: Early to midsummer

Habitat/Range: Moist woods, thickets, and openings at low to mid elevations on the west side of the Cascades.

Comments: *Polemonium* is from a Greek medicinal plant often associated with the philosopher, Polemon. *Carneum* ("flesh-colored") refers to the flowers. Jacob's Ladder *(P. pulcherrimum)* is smaller and with bluish white, funnel-shaped flowers. Flies and bees are common pollinators of the flowers.

GLOSSARY

Alternate—placed singly along a stem or axis, one after another, usually each successive item on a different side from the previous; often used in reference to the arrangement of leaves on a stem (*see* Opposite).

Annual—a plant completing its life cycle, from seed germination to production of new seeds, within a year, and then dying.

Axil—the area created on the upper side of the angle between a leaf and stem.

Basal—at the base or bottom of; generally used in reference to leaves arranged at the base of the plant.

Biennial—a plant completing its life cycle in two years, and normally not producing flowers during the first year.

Bract—reduced or modified leaf, often associated with flowers.

Bristle—a stiff hair, usually erect or curving away from its attachment point.

Bulb—underground plant part derived from a short, usually rounded, shoot that is covered with scales or leaves.

Calyx—the outer set of flower parts, composed of the sepals, which may be separate or joined together; usually green.

Capsule—a dry fruit that releases seeds through splits or holes.

Compound Leaf—a leaf that is divided into two to many leaflets, each of which may look like a complete leaf, but which lacks buds. Compound leaves may have leaflets arranged along an axis like the rays of a feather or radiating from a common point like the fingers on a hand (*see* illustration p. 9).

Corolla—the set of flower parts interior to the calyx and surrounding the stamens, composed of the petals, which may be free or united; often brightly colored.

Deciduous—referring to broad-leaved trees or shrubs that drop their leaves at the end of each growing season, as contrasted with plants that retain the leaves throughout the year (*see* Evergreen).

Disk Flowers—small, tubular flowers in the central portion of the flower head of many plants in the Sunflower Family (Asteraceae) (*see* illustration p. 11).

Elliptical (Leaf Shape)—*see* illustration p. 10.

Entire (Leaf Margin)—*see* illustration p. 9.

Evergreen—referring to plants that bear green leaves throughout the year, as contrasted with plants that lose their leaves at the end of the growing season (*see* Deciduous).

Family—a group of plants having biologically similar features, such as flower anatomy, fruit type, etc.

Flower Head—as used in this guide, a dense and continuous group of flowers, without obvious branches or space between them; used especially in reference to the Sunflower Family (Asteraceae).

Genus—a group of closely related species, such as the genus *Penstemon* encompassing the penstemons (*see* Specific Epithet).

Herbaceous—refering to any nonwoody plant; often reserved for wildflowers.

Hood—curving or folded, petal-like structure interior to the petals and exterior to the stamens in the Milkweed Family (Asclepiadaceae); since most milkweeds have reflexed petals, the hoods are typically the most prominent feature of the flowers.

Inflorescence—generally a cluster of flowers, although there are many terms to specifically describe the arrangement of flowers on the plant.

Involucre—a distinct series of bracts or leaves that subtend a flower or cluster of flowers. Often used in the description of the Sunflower Family (Asteraceae) flower heads.

Keel—a sharp lengthwise fold or ridge, referring particularly to the two fused petals forming the lower lip in many flowers of the Pea Family (Fabaceae).

Lance (Leaf Shape)—*see* illustration p. 10.

Leaflet—a distinct, leaflike segment of a compound leaf.

Linear (Leaf Shape)—*see* illustration p. 10.

Lobe—a segment of an incompletely divided plant part, typically rounded; often used in reference to the leaves.

Midrib—the central or main vein of a leaf.

Node—the region of the stem where one or more leaves are attached. Buds are commonly borne at the node, in the axils of the leaves.

Nutlet—a descriptive term for small nutlike fruits. Used to describe the separate lobes of a mature ovary in the Borage (Boraginaceae) and Mint (Laminaceae) families.

Oblong (Leaf Shape)—*see* illustration p. 10.

Opposite—paired directly across from one another along a stem or axis (*see* Alternate).

Ovary—the portion of the flower where the seeds develop, usually a swollen area below the style (if present) and stigma.

Pappus—in the Sunflower Family (Asteraceae), the modified limb of the calyx is the pappus, which consists of a crown of bristles, hairs, or scales at the top of the seed.

Parallel—side by side, approximately the same distance apart for the entire length; often used in reference to veins or edges of leaves.

Perennial—a plant that normally lives for three or more years.

Petal—component part of the corolla, often the most brightly colored and visible part of the flower.

Petiole—the stalk of a leaf. The length of the petiole may be used in leaf descriptions.

Pinnate—referring to a compound leaf, like many of the Pea Family (Fabaceae) members, where smaller leaflets are arranged along either side of a common axis.

Pistil—the seed-producing, or female, part of a flower, consisting of the ovary, style (if present), and stigma; a flower may have one to several separate pistils.

Pollen—tiny, often powdery male reproductive cells formed in the stamens and typically necessary for seed production.

Ray Flower—flower in the Sunflower Family (Asteraceae) with a single, strap-shaped corolla, resembling one flower petal; several to many ray flowers may surround the disk flowers in a flower head, or in some species such as dandelions, the flower heads may be composed entirely of ray flowers (*see* illustration p. 11).

Rosette—a dense cluster of basal leaves from a common underground part, often in a flattened, circular arrangement.

Scale—any thin, membranous body that somewhat resembles the scales of fish or reptiles.

Sepal—component part of the calyx; typically green but sometimes enlarged and brightly colored.

Shrub—a perennial woody plant of relatively low height, and typically with several stems arising from or near the ground.

Simple Leaf—a leaf that has a single leaflike blade, although this may be lobed or divided.

Spatula (Leaf Shape)—*see* illustration p. 10.

Specific Epithet—the second portion of a scientific name, identifying a particular species; for instance in Tiger Lily, *Lilium columbianum,* the specific epithet is *"columbianum."*

Spike—an elongate, unbranched cluster of stalkless or nearly stalkless flowers.

Stalk—as used here, the stem supporting the leaf, flower, or flower cluster.

Stalkless—lacking a stalk; a stalkless leaf is attached directly to the stem at the leaf base.

Stamen—the male unit of a flower, which produces the pollen; typically consisting of a long filament with a pollen-producing tip.

Standard—the usually erect, spreading upper petal in many flowers of the Pea Family (Fabaceae).

Stigma—portion of the pistil receptive to pollination; usually at the top of the style, and often appearing fuzzy or sticky.

Style—the portion of the pistil between the ovary and the stigma; typically a slender stalk.

Subtend—to be situated below or beneath, often encasing or enclosing something.

Toothed—bearing teeth, or sharply angled projections, along the edge.

Variety—a group of plants within a species that has a distinct range, habitat, or structure.

Whorl—three or more parts attached at the same point along a stem or axis and often surrounding the stem.

Wings—the two side petals flanking the keel in many flowers of the Pea Family (Fabaceae).

SELECTED REFERENCES

Barth, Friedrich G. *Insects and Flowers: The Biology of a Partnership.* Princeton, N.J.:
Princeton University Press, 1985.

Chipman, Art. *Wildflower Trails of the Pacific Northwest.* Medford, Ore.: Pine Cone Publishers, 1970.

Coombes, Allen J. *Dictionary of Plant Names.* Portland, Ore.: Timber Press, Inc., 1994.

Cronquist, A., A. Holmgren, N.H. Holmgren, J.L. Reveal, P.K. Holmgren, and R.C. Barneby.
Intermountain Flora, Vascular Plants of the Intermountain West, U.S.A., vols. 3–6. New
York: The New York Botanical Garden, 1977–97.

Durrant, Mary. *Who Named the Daisy? Who Named the Rose?* New York: Dodd, Mead and
Company, 1976.

Gilkey, Helen M. and La Rea J. Dennis. *Handbook of Northwestern Plants,* rev. ed. Oregon
State University Press, Corvallis, 2001.

Haskin, Leslie L. *Wild Flowers of the Pacific Coast.* Portland, Ore.: Binfords & Mort, Publishers, 1967.

Hitchcock, C.L., and A. Cronquist. *Flora of the Pacific Northwest.* Seattle: University of
Washington Press, 1973.

Horn, Elizabeth L. *Coastal Wildflowers of the Pacific Northwest.* Missoula, Mont.: Mountain Press Publishing Co., 1993.

Ireland, Orlin L. *Plants of the Three Sisters Region, Oregon Cascade Range.* Eugene, Ore.:
Bull. No. 12, University of Oregon, 1968.

Jolley, Russ. *Wildflowers of the Columbia River Gorge.* Portland, Ore.: Oregon Historical
Society Press, 1988.

Kleinman, Kathryn and Sara Slavin. *On Flowers.* San Francisco: Chronicle Books, 1992.

Kozloff, Eugene N. *Plants and Animals of the Pacific Northwest: An Illustrated Guide to the
Natural History of Western Oregon, Washington, and British Columbia.* Seattle: University of Washington Press, 1976.

Larrison, E.J., G.W. Patrick, W.H. Baker, and J.A. Yaich. *Washington Wildflowers.* Seattle:
The Seattle Audubon Society, 1974.

Lyons, C.P. *Wildflowers of Washington.* Vancouver, British Columbia: Lone Pine Publishing,
1999.

Mathews, Daniel A. *Cascade-Olympic Natural History.* Portland, Ore.: Raven Editions, 1988.

Meeuse, Bastiaan and Sean Morris. *The Sex Life of Flowers.* New York: Facts on File Publications, 1984.

Moulton, Gary E., ed. *Journals of the Lewis and Clark Expedition.* 12 vols. Lincoln, Neb.: University of Nebraska Press, 1983–99.

Nicholls, Graham. *Alpine Plants of North America: An Encyclopedia of Mountain Flowers from the Rockies to Alaska.* Portland, Ore.: Timber Press, Inc., 2002.

Parish, Roberta, Ray Coupé and Dennis Lloyd, eds. *Plants of Southern Interior British Columbia and the Inland Northwest.* Vancouver, British Columbia: Lone Pine Publishing, 1996.

Phillips, H. Wayne. *Plants of the Lewis & Clark Expedition.* Missoula, Mont.: Mountain Press Publishing Co., 2003.

Pojar, Jim and Andy MacKinnon. *Plants of the Pacific Northwest Coast: Washington, Oregon, British Columbia & Alaska.* Vancouver, British Columbia: Lone Pine Publishing, 1994.

Proctor, M. Peter Yeo and Andrew Lack. *The Natural History of Pollination.* Portland, Ore.: Timber Press, Inc., 1996.

Ross, Robert A. and Henrietta L. *Chambers. Wildflowers of the Western Cascades.* Portland, Ore.: Timber Press, Inc., 1988.

Saling, Ann. *The Great Northwest Nature Factbook: Remarkable animals, plants & natural features in Washington, Oregon, Idaho & Montana.* Bothell, Wash.: Alaska Northwest Books, 1991.

Sanders, Jack. *Hedgemaids and Fairy Candles: The Lives and Lore of North American Wildflowers.* Camden, Maine: Ragged Mountain Press, 1993.

Snowdon, Lord. *Wild Flowers.* New York: Clarkson Potter Publishers, 1995.

Stearn, William T. *Stearn's Dictionary of Plant Names for Gardeners.* Portland, Ore.: Timber Press, Inc., 1996.

Strickler, Dr. Dee. *Wayside Wildflowers of the Pacific Northwest.* Columbia Falls, Mont.: The Falcon Press, 1993.

Taylor, Ronald J. *Sagebrush Country: A Wildflower Sanctuary.* Missoula, Mont.: Mountain Press Publishing Co., 1992.

___and George W. Douglas. *Mountain Plants of the Pacific Northwest.* Missoula, Mont.: Mountain Press Publishing Co., 1995.

___*Mountain Wild Flowers of the Pacific Northwest.* Portland, Ore.: Binford & Mort, Publishers, 1975.

Terrill, Steve. *Wildflowers of Oregon.* Englewood, Colo.: Westcliff Publishers, Inc., 1995.

Whitney, Stephen R. and Rob Sandelin. *Field Guide to the Cascades & Olympics.* Seattle: The Mountaineer Books, 2003.

Wuerthner, George. *Oregon's Best Wildflower Hikes: Northwest Region.* Englewood, Colo.: Westcliff Publishers, Inc., 2001.

Web Sites

Burke Museum, http//:biology.burke.washington.edu/herbarium/imagecollections/list.php

California Flora, www.caflora.org

Checklist of the Vascular Flora of Oregon, www.swsbm.com

Northwest Native Plant Journal, www.nwplants.com

Pacific Northwest Wildflower Bloom Reports,
    http//:ghs.gresham.k12.or.us/science/ps/nature/bloomtime

Washington Native Plant Society, www.wnps.org

INDEX

ABOUT THE AUTHOR

Damian Fagan graduated from the University of Washington in 1982 with a B.S. in Botany. He has worked for the Seattle City Parks and National Park Service as a naturalist and ranger; as a contract wildlife biologist; and as a program manager for The Nature Conservancy. His writing and photography credits include newspapers, magazines, and calendars. This is his third book credit for The Globe Pequot Press, the first two being: *Canyon Country Wildflowers* (author/photographer) and *Yosemite On My Mind* (text researcher). He resides in central Oregon with his family.